"Seldom has an author gone skillfully and incisively as ha. for Eden. *With powerful use of metaphor, wit, and personal experience, the reader is enticed to join a pilgrimage of spiritual formation and personal sanctification. You will laugh, cry, and grow. You will underscore line after line for reprise in moments of reflection."*

DONALD S. AULTMAN, ED. D.
PRESIDENT, PSYCHOLOGICAL STUDIES INSTITUTE

"This is a book that will at once both stimulate spiritual hunger and satisfy it. Gary Moon writes with a style that is fresh and clear, and the book reveals a voice that is personal and engaging. The overall metaphor of the spiritual journey as a return home is wonderfully rich, reflecting not only the author's own spiritual pilgrimage but also the longing of many of us. Consequently, I predict that this book will be extremely well received, and I heartily recommend it to anyone who wishes to better understand his own yearning to return to Eden and the spiritual journey this involves."

DAVID BENNER, PH. D.
AUTHOR OF *PSYCHOTHERAPY AND THE SPIRITUAL QUEST*,
AND EDITOR OF THE *BAKER ENCYCLOPEDIA OF PSYCHOLOGY*
PROFESSOR OF PSYCHOLOGY, REDEEMER COLLEGE, ONTARIO

"Drawing on creativity and counseling experience, Gary Moon has written a captivating, perceptive, and insightful critique of the field of counseling (and its potential for integration with Christian spiritual direction). Homesick for Eden *is worth reading and pondering deeply.'*

GARY R. COLLINS, PH. D.
PRESIDENT OF THE AMERICAN ASSOCIATION
OF CHRISTIAN COUNSELORS

"In Homesick for Eden *the reader is provided an essential synthesis of psychotherapy and spiritual direction. With a fair and balanced hand, the author returns therapy to its graceful roots—the*

care of the soul. I recommend it heartily for all those who desire soul-healing."

CAPT. DONALD B. HARRIS, M. DIV.
FOUNDER OF CREDO INTERNATIONAL AND NAVY CREDO

"*In* Homesick for Eden, *Gary Moon knits modern psychotherapy and ancient spiritual direction into his tapestry of present-day 'soulology.' I found myself in every chapter and was inspired to take another leap of faith and action. A delightful and courageous book.*"

LES PARROTT III, PH. D.
AUTHOR OF *HIGH MAINTENANCE RELATIONSHIPS*
ASSOCIATE PROFESSOR OF PSYCHOLOGY
SEATTLE PACIFIC UNIVERSITY

"Homesick for Eden *is a beautifully written book that describes and illustrates from personal and other examples, eight major steps or leaps in Christian spirituality — leaps necessary for life in the kingdom of God. It will help you and touch your life deeply. I recommend it most highly!*"

SIANG-YANG TAN, PH. D.
AUTHOR (WITH JOHN ORTBERG) OF
UNDERSTANDING DEPRESSION
DIRECTOR OF THE PSY. D. PROGRAM AND
ASSOCIATE PROFESSOR OF PSYCHOLOGY,
GRADUATE SCHOOL OF PSYCHOLOGY
FULLER THEOLOGICAL SEMINARY

"*The 20th century's discovery of the seamless unity between psychological maturation and spiritual sanctification has transformed the hoary disciplines of spiritual direction and jump-started the latter into the forefront of human development. Gary Moon's* Homesick for Eden *is surely 'Exhibit A.' Written with charm, simplicity, and wit, it will lead even beginners into depths of psyche and spirit they would have thought unattainable.*"

THE REVEREND CANON GRAY TEMPLE, JR.
RECTOR, ST. PATRICK'S EPISCOPAL CHURCH
ATLANTA, GEORGIA

"What a delightful book. Gary Moon has done a superb job of communicating some profound truths in a way that anybody can understand and learn. His personal odyssey is revealed in the many anecdotes from his life experience. But the truths which he has personally discovered are carefully etched in the book. Insights from modern psychotherapy help to extenuate some of the deepest realities of spiritual formation. I would encourage every Christian who desires a wholesome relationship with God to read Homesick for Eden."

REVEREND B. E. UNDERWOOD
BISHOP, INTERNATIONAL PENTECOSTAL HOLINESS CHURCH
AUTHOR OF *PORTRAIT OF A PASTOR*

"In a day of high stress and desperate need for inner resources to cope, Homesick for Eden *is a book that indeed offers practical insight for spiritual living in a secularized society. In the 'eight-giant-leaps' Gary Moon provides an excellent ministry source for counselors, pastors, church leaders, and lay people alike.*"

REVEREND PAUL L. WALKER, PH. D.
GENERAL OVERSEER CHURCH OF GOD
PASTOR EMERITUS MOUNT PARAN CHURCH OF GOD

"Homesick for Eden *is a charmingly honest and painstakingly detailed look at the torn condition of human beings, the religious ones included. The author sees into the soul and then deftly shows how to unsnarl the lines of communication and influence that open us up to God. His gentle and humorous style holds the reader close while conveying the deepest of spiritual lessons.*"

DALLAS WILLARD, PH. D.
AUTHOR OF *THE SPIRIT OF DISCIPLINES*
PROFESSOR OF PHILOSOPHY
UNIVERSITY OF SOUTHERN CALIFORNIA

" *The Spirit is awakening our culture to a distinct Christian understanding of the soul. Gary Moon's book is an important contribution in this awakening. For every 10 books I red one resonates with the core of my heart. This is that one book.*"

DR. LARRY CRAGG
AUTHOR, PSYCHOLOGIST, AND DISTINGUISHED SCHOLAR IN RESIDENCE
AT COLORADO CHRISTIAN UNIVERSITY

HOMESICK FOR EDEN

A Soul's Journey to Joy

GARY W. MOON

SERVANT PUBLICATIONS
ANN ARBOR, MICHIGAN

Vine Books is an imprint of Servant Publications especially designed to serve evangelical Christians.

Although the stories in this book are true, all names and identifying characteristics have been changed to protect the privacy of those involved.

Published by Servant Publications
P.O. Box 8617
Ann Arbor, Michigan 48107

Cover design: Left Coast Design, Portland, Oregon
Cover illustration: Leslie Wu. Used by permission.

97 98 99 00 10 9 8 7 6 5 4 3 2 1

Printed in the United States of America
ISBN 1-56955-050-6

LIBRARY OF CONGRESS CATALOGING-IN-PUBLICATION DATA

Moon, Gary W.
Homesick for Eden : a soul's journey to joy / Gary W. Moon.
    p.   cm.
Originally published : Franklin, Ga. : LifeSprings Resources, 1996.
Includes bibliographical references.
ISBN 1-56955-050-6
1. Spiritual life—Christianity.   2. Moon, Gary W., 1956-   .   I Title.
[BV4501.2.M573   1997]
248.4—dc21   97-9263
                                                               CIP

To Regina, my wife and best friend.

To Jesse and Jenna
who cause me to believe in the miraculous, every day.

To the friends who helped to write this book through hundreds of coffee-shop conversations: Marty, Jay, Steve, Rob, Bill, Greg, Clarence, and Harold.

To Lewis Grizzard who unknowingly convinced me
that people might be interested in the
life-stories of a small town southern boy;
and who taught me how to write
through my reading and re-reading of his story of a life.

CONTENTS

Here thou hast no abiding city;
and wherever thou shalt be, thou art a stranger
and a pilgrim; nor wilt thou ever have rest
except thou be united with Christ.

THOMAS Á KEMPIS

Ever since God expelled Adam and Eve from the garden, we have lived in an unnatural environment—a world in which we were not designed to live. We were built to enjoy a garden without weeds, relationships without friction, fellowship without distance. But something is wrong and we know it, both within our world and within ourselves. Deep inside we sense we're out of the nest, always ending the day in a motel room and never at home.

LARRY CRABB
INSIDE OUT

Introduction

It wasn't until the second day of my imprisonment that it hit me like a punch, right to the stomach. The blow left me dazed. All I knew for sure was that I was sick, really sick, and that I had to get out of that room.

It must have been a very small room, because even back then—when I was only eight years old, I still remember the cold, blank stare of those four cinder-block walls, and I remember their color. The walls had been painted with a thin layer of that disgusting shade of green that no one ever buys. That putrid hue that always ends up being given away to some institution, because it looks so much like the contents of a sick stomach.

There were no decorations on those walls, and no sheets or blankets on the other bunk-bed to hide an assortment of ancient stains. The furniture was simple, old, and mostly broken. It was as if a Kmart had exploded in an army barracks. And I was sitting in the middle of it.

The room, however, was in a lot better shape than I was. I lay on my back, rolling from side to side, and moaning. I didn't have a fever. I wasn't covered with spots, or welts, or scabs, or anything else which would provide concrete evidence that I needed attention. I was simply sick. If loneliness could fester up into fitful desperation and had a name, then I could have told someone what kind of sick I was.

Hours later, one of the "guards" finally heard my groans. He stood over my bed and said, "Aw, you're just homesick. Don't worry. You'll get over it. Just hang in there." But, I didn't get over it. And I decided not to hang in there.

Later that day, when the shadows were long and the color in the trees and bushes had bled into gray, I decided to make a break for it. I snuck out of my room, and down two flights of metal stairs on the outside of the building. I crept across the grounds of the compound, sticking close to the bushes and staying in the oversized shadows, like I had seen James West do in *The Wild, Wild West* (my favorite TV show at the time). Then, when the time was just right, I darted out the main entrance.

I followed the path of a major highway, and wondered frequently if the passersby knew what I had just done. I wondered if they would call the authorities. I finally approached safety. I had almost completed the long trek. With a weary arm and trembling knuckles, I knocked on a big white door and heard the familiar sound of brisk footsteps on a plastic runner. The door creaked open and revealed the surprised face of my mother. She exclaimed, "Gary, why aren't you at youth camp?"

"I was homesick," I said.

In the years that followed, my size two shoes were not the only things I outgrew; eventually I outgrew getting homesick. However, once in a while I wondered if I might relapse. Perhaps that was because my initial bout had been so severe. Perhaps that's why I never joined the Peace Corps, the Marine Corps, or any other corps.

It was a long time—many years and a few joyful months into a six-year hitch in graduate school, that one day I let out a deep sigh as I realized, *truly realized*, I had finally licked that "just-homesick" disease. I was 2,300 miles from that camp, and I knew I would never again experience those horrible sensations.

For a long, long time, I was all right. Then one evening those same old feelings hit me again; this time like two jabs to the stomach and a head-butt to the nose. I was homesick again and I knew it. After all, I had been a poster child for the disease.

There I was, a twenty-nine-year-old man with a wonderful wife and a two-year-old daughter. I had picked up a Ph.D. in clinical psychology, and an M.Div. in theology during those six years of graduate school. Why, I was even sitting on the very same steps to the house where I had fled as a homesick eight-year-old! *And I was feeling it again!*

This time, however, I wasn't homesick for my family home. I was sitting on the front steps of my family home. I was homesick for my *real* home. I was homesick for the kingdom of heaven, for the lost Eden. Somehow I knew, at the deepest level possible, that I was a long, long way from the "garden" that I'd been designed for. I knew that I was tired of living out of a suitcase, and I wanted to go back home.

From rat mazes to Rogers, I had studied the modern discipline which should have helped me at a time like this. I was a psychologist. From Jesus to Jung, I'd learned the ancient disciplines of soul care. From youth camp to Bible college I had followed the advice of evangelists. I had been born again so many times my soul had stretch marks. But I had no experiential knowledge, no personal experience with the kingdom of heaven. The concept of abundant life was nothing more to me than words on the pages of *Kittel's Exhaustive Word Study Encyclopedia*.

I sat there with my posterior pressing into the concrete steps of home dripping tears onto my scribbling. I filled page after page of a yellow tablet with words that sprang from the deepest crannies of my heart. "Where is the kingdom?", "Where is abundant life?", "Why am I the only one that seems to be having stomach cramps over the situation?"

I had read enough to suspect that I was feeling what St. Augustine must have felt when he penned, "My soul finds no rest until it rests in Thee;" and enough to suppose that what I was feeling was what Jung had declared: that after age thirty-five all problems are spiritual problems. Perhaps I had finally reached one of the developmental milestones of life and thus my confusion.

I had been to enough churches to realize that I did not need to keep looking for a better flock, or a better shepherd. I needed to be home. I wanted to hear God's brisk footsteps on a celestial, plastic carpet-protector, and see his surprised look as he said, "Gary, why aren't you still in life camp?"

While it was hard to resist, I didn't sneak off that night to look for Eden. I knew that there was nowhere to look but deep within. I did resolve in that moment of looking within to spend a lifetime searching, if that's what it would take to find it.

During the next twelve months I continued my introspection and I filled hundreds of journal pages. Just for good measure, I also searched outside my being. I traveled thousands of miles to visit scores of retreat centers—places that suggested pathways to Eden.

Somewhere along the way, I believe that God gave me a "pillar of fire" to guide my search. I found it in the form of an analogy about the roles of psychotherapy and spiritual direction when one is searching for paradises lost. From that moment on, I always kept that pillar in view.

That year of very active searching came to a merciful end when our bank balance read "0." I began a private practice, and quickly discovered I was not alone in my search for Eden. The majority of clients I worked with were as homesick as I was. Of course, I never let on to them that I was searching, too. Eventually, over dozens of "power-lunches" and "thank-you-for-the-referral-breakfasts," I also discovered that the majority of pastors and physicians who were referring clients to me were equally homesick. Mercifully, some of them made it all the way back. There they heard the comforting voice of their real parent, their Father, saying, "I'm so glad you made it back to your real home—to Eden."

I hope you enjoy a story about a good homecoming, because that's what this book is about. And I hope it makes you really homesick, too—homesick for the world for which you were designed, a world of fellowship without distance, a world where perfect love pins perfect fear to the mat.

Before You Start

This is not a traditional self-help book. If it were, it would have been divided into parts with headings such as: "Why Am I Hurting?"; "Who Can Help Me?" "The Limits of Psychology"; "Beyond Psychology"; and "The Benefits of Spiritual Direction." The "spiritual direction" section would likely have been divided into eight chapters with titles like: "Living in the Kingdom of God"; "Learning to Practice His Presence"; "How to Hear His Voice"; "Becoming Willing When Willful Feels More Natural"; "Overcoming Your Deepest Fears and Idols"; "Purgation—The Hurt That Heals"; "Forgiveness—Caster Oil for Emotions"; and "Reconciliation with God." But this book is not about all of that—at least not in such clean categories.

What this book is, is a non-traditional, God-help-me, story-book. While all of the above topics are addressed between these covers, this does not happen in a precise, linear fashion. They are embedded in the stories of others, my autobiography, fables, and analogies, in the same order that they were "accidentally" discovered by the people you are about to meet.

Perhaps I have heard one too many "How to be a mature Christian" presentations where each of the "how to's" started with the same letter of the alphabet. Perhaps I was dropped on my head at a critical time of development, or maybe I am simply a frustrated storyteller. Whatever the case, I felt it was more true to life to present these tales of personal Christian formation in the same manner in which they were discovered.

After all, I suspect that if any orderly path to spiritual maturity could be presented, Jesus would have pulled out a study guide, instead of telling parables and making himself a living lesson.

My hope for you, dear reader, is that you will come along for the ride, and that you will not get off this ride until you find yourself several "giant leaps" closer to Eden than when you first got on. But we still have a problem to deal with. Because the stories that follow are, uh, stories, I thought it might prove helpful to provide an "advanced organizer" so that if you ever find yourself mid-fable, and begin to wonder how the experiences of a particular character relate to the overall journey back home to Eden, you can flip back to the paragraphs that follow to get your bearings.

Advanced Organizer

Chapter One

Chapter one presents two parables which are foundational to the intent and organization of the book. The first story of Plato's Cave is told to help us distinguish between the "world" where we presently toil (the cave) and the "kingdom" that we are invited to enjoy.

The second parable involves the journey of "Adam," who could be any one of us. He finds himself homesick and a long way from Eden. Four individuals—three psychologists and a spiritual director—help him. All four offer good advice, but only one of them helps him get back to the open arms of his father.

Chapter Two

In this chapter, the second parable is unpacked. The first three helpers are identified as representatives of behavioral, cognitive, and existential psychology. And here Adam's problems, that are universal to mankind, are presented. They are:

- compassion deficit,
- over-use of behavioral narcotics,
- and the problem of having a true and a false self behind the wheel of his life.

An ancient fable from Jewish folklore is told here, as well as the story of a modern-day Adam along with *his* compassion deficits, behavioral narcotics, two selves, and his encounters with the first three helpers.

Chapter Three

The fourth helper, a spiritual director, is reintroduced along with his "Eight Giant Leaps in Christian Formation" program. Now, the story of the modern-day Adam, begun in chapter two, is completed.

Chapter Four

Throughout the rest of the book, the reader is invited into the counseling room to sit with the author as he meets a series of people who are making the same pilgrimage that Adam in chapter one and the modern-day Adam of chapters two and three made. The reader is also invited to wade around in the author's stream of consciousness as the reader begins to wonder about his own travel plans.

Bill is the first client whose story is told, and Bill receives help from the first three of the four helpers.

Chapter Five

Diane's story is told. She decides to climb on board with the hermit (the fourth helper) for a while, before a "sea monster" appears and blocks the way to Eden.

Chapter Six

Here is Janet's story. She also receives help from the first three psychological helpers, and then from the hermit (the spiritual director). Janet successfully navigates the trip back home to Eden.

Chapter Seven

The author completes his own story which was begun in chapter four. He describes his travels from psychology to spiritual direction, and from life in Plato's Cave to the kingdom. It plays in Peoria.

So there you have it. This book is about an ancient journey—the journey from Egypt (the world) to the land of milk and honey (the promised land of the kingdom of God). It's as difficult to navigate the journey now as it was three millennia ago.

While I have avoided like the plague (no pun intended), drawing a precise road map, I do believe that the following pages document the promises and pitfalls of several "giant leaps" of faith necessary to navigate the wilderness.

I hope it makes you want to pack your bags and head for Eden.

1

A Tell Of Two Tales

Earth's crammed with heaven
And every common bush afire with God.
But only he who sees takes off his shoes—
The rest sit around it
and pluck blackberries.

Elizabeth Barrett Browning

You just never know when some really profound thought is going to walk up to you and say hello. I know a thought gave me a pretty heavy howdy once, when it was least expected.

It was a springtime Saturday morning, and I was sitting in a converted Sunday school classroom in the underbelly of a large church in southern California. The four walls were brightly decorated with cardboard cutouts of smiling disciples and a laughing Jesus. I assumed it would be filled with a pack of energetic five-year-olds the next morning. But it was Saturday, and the crowd I was with was not that young or bubbly. I was sitting with forty other frowning, dully-decorated, jeans-clad seminarians. From the collective countenance, it appeared that each preferred to be anywhere else. I was surprised Jesus kept smiling.

I was there because I needed one last theology class to graduate. Because that particular course was not offered at the main campus, I was faced with a ninety-minute drive to an 8 A.M. class at that remote seminary outpost. It looked as if everyone else were in the same boat.

The professor entered the room. He was smiling so broadly that he seemed to belong up on the wall with Jesus and the disciples, instead of down on the tile floor with the rest of us. He started unpacking his briefcase, surrounding himself with orderly piles of books and folders. He didn't need to go to all that trouble for me. I could already tell him what I wanted from the course. I wanted the words of his lecture notes to be transferred to my blank, yellow legal pad, and then back onto his final exam paper in the most painless way possible. I didn't care if his lecture ever made it into my head.

His methodical search led him to a video tape. He seemed very pleased with the find and placed it in the appropriate machine, turned the lights off and the volume up. Within seconds crudely drawn animated figures were peering at us from the TV screen. Life was as it should be. It was Saturday morning and I was watching cartoons.

But it wasn't Pluto. It was Plato. To be more precise, it was Platos Cave. Still, I wasn't complaining.

Tale One: The Cave and the Kingdom

The audio sounded like a cat whose voice was changing. The drawings were worse than you would expect from a three-year-old Walt Disney. But the content was mesmerizing.

The camera focused first on the faces of four prisoners. They were laughing and pointing straight ahead. Then, the camera panned backward and revealed that each prisoner was bound by chains in such a manner that it would be impossible for him to stand or to look behind.

The men we saw were prisoners who lived in a large underground cave. The only thing they were allowed to see was the back wall of their Flintstonian home.

Behind them, at the mouth of the cave a huge fire burned. It threw light against the wall they faced.

On a raised platform between the fire and the prisoners, people marched back and forth carrying wooden carvings of objects—trees, flowers, birds, and the like—high over their heads. These people were too far away for their voices or footsteps to be clearly heard.

The objects that were paraded in front of the fire caused shadows to be cast on the back wall screen, making the prisoners a captive theater audience with no popcorn.

The shadows on the wall of the cave were the only reality the prisoners knew. And as one might expect, they had made a contest of naming the shadows and predicting the patterns of their appearance. The prisoners became quite good at these interpretations and predictions. Indeed, they adopted the custom of offering an award to the one who was best at the game.

Then one day (of course the cell mates knew nothing of the concept of day) someone entered the cave and descended to where the prisoners were kept in a single-file, shoulder-to-shoulder row. He approached them, knelt behind one, touched his chains, and they fell to the floor. The now-freed prisoner awkwardly stood to his feet. The one who had done the freeing attempted to explain about the cave and the outside world. But it was difficult to communicate with someone who could speak only shadowese.

Reluctantly, the former prisoner allowed himself to be led up the steep ascent to the mouth of the cave, where upon arrival, he grabbed his eyes in pain because of the brightness of the sun. He had never seen it before and its burning reality caused his eyes to squint and his eyelids to slam shut. He had to be held to be kept from running back to the safety of the dark cave. He did not realize he was a butterfly, finally set free from a cocoon.

In time, however, he slowly adapted to the light. It wasn't long before he was able to see real trees, flowers, and birds. And, in even less time, the truth began to dawn on him. His world had been a prison which contained only the shadows of reality, the reality of life-in-full.

The former prisoner began to run and play like an excited child. He put his feet in real water, inhaled the fragrance of real flowers, and heard the melody of a choir of real birds. For the first time ever, he was filled with joy. That is, until he remembered the other three prisoners.

Compassion propelled him back to the entrance of the cave. He decided that he must again descend into his former dwelling and help free the others, even though he hated to miss one moment in the real world.

When he arrived back in their presence, it was readily apparent to all of them there that he had changed. He had grown accustomed to the outside world, to light, and to freedom. The shadows on the wall appeared fuzzy to him now, and he had forgotten the games of trivial pursuit—predicting the shadow patterns.

The others saw his difficulty and concluded that he was mad. Instead of welcoming his offer of freedom, they laughed at the messenger and decided that he should be put to death. Fortunately for him, they were chained. With slow steps the would-be-messiah left the jeering captives and ascended again to the real world, thinking to himself, "Better to be the poor servant of a poor master (outside the cave) than to think and live as they."

The projector sputtered to a stop and the professor turned the lights back on in our cave. He asked only, "So, what do you think?"

While others came to life and responded for almost an hour, I sat in stunned silence as an internal documentary was filmed on location, in my head.

What did I think? I thought that I had just sat in a twentieth-century church and witnessed the telling of a pre-Christian parable by a troupe of cartoon figures which caused a floodlight bulb to turn on in my mind. The life and the mission of Christ had finally become illuminated.

From the Garden of Eden to Plato's Cave

How had I missed all the cave and kingdom language in Scripture? Didn't Jesus begin his earthly ministry with the announcement that he had entered into our cave (the world) to set captives free, to restore sight to the blind, to proclaim the good news that there is another world all around us and it is called the kingdom of God? The contrast between the world (the cave) and the kingdom had never been drawn so clearly for me.

Other parallels began to pop in my mind like flashbulbs: Jesus, put to death by those whose secure reality was challenged by his talk of the outside world of his kingdom; Nobel Prizes being as inconsequential as the awards given for shadow-interpreter-of-the-year; that there actually was here-and-now good news in the gospel of Jesus.

But then the really big insight hit. It was such a blow that I could almost feel a cartoon-sized knot growing from the top of my head.

In the Christian experience, it is possible to be set free from our chains, and yet never leave the cave. Perhaps we fear the journey. Perhaps the pain caused by the first beams of sunlight is too intense. Perhaps we never got a good AAA atlas or a mentor (spiritual director) for the trip. Often we live our lives more in line with the principles of the cave (earthly shadow-games of politics, power, and material securities) rather than those of the kingdom (simplicity, willingness, selfless love).

Other than adding a cross shadow to the shadow interpretation games, and having a better after-life retirement plan, it is often hard to tell the difference between Christians and prisoners in the cave of this world.

Yes, I thought, we have indeed fallen from the Garden of Eden into Plato's cave. We live in an unnatural environment, one for which we were not designed. And for all the talk of abundant life and the kingdom of God, our reality is most often, that of rock and shadow.

I would like to go outside now, I continued to think. Not outside the classroom; outside the cave. I looked up at the cardboard cutout of Jesus and the disciples. So that's why they're all smiling! There really is something to be joyful about. As I thought that, I'm pretty sure I saw Jesus wink.

Tale Two: The Long Row Home

In Plato's Cave I had discovered a treasure trove. And in the months that followed, I found new riches in the reading of old Scripture.

The words Jesus had borrowed from Isaiah to announce the beginning of his mission on earth took on greater, how-could-I-possibly-have-missed-that clarity.

> The Spirit of the Lord is upon me,
> because he has anointed me
> to bring glad tidings to the poor.
> He has sent me to proclaim liberty to captives
> and recovery of sight to the blind,
> to let the oppressed go free,
> and to proclaim a year acceptable to the Lord.
>
> LUKE 4:18-19.

I was left to wonder however, have I truly been set free, or am I still blind to the truth of life outside the cave?

I soon finished that last theology class, and with it my formal education in theology. I had already finished a doctoral program in clinical psychology.

It was time to begin a practice as a psychologist, to start shoveling money into the student loan repayment program.

But there was a problem: I felt a much stronger urging to do the work of spiritual direction (helping others find the way out of the cave) than to do the work of a clinical psychologist (attending to the wounds of the captives). And there was an additional problem: I didn't know the way out of the cave myself. I had simply become convinced that finding the way out was the here-and-now good news of the gospel.

Then one day, while putting off getting a real job, driving on a numberless back road in Wisconsin, a story popped into my head. Once again I was surprised by a "hello there" from a profound spiritual thought, and I wasn't even a vegetarian.

This is how it went.

Adam's Unhelpful Helpers

Once upon a time, a man not-so-coincidentally named Adam, awoke from a long nap to find himself in a small rowboat, riding through a pea-soup fog, on the aqua-blue backs of slow-rolling waves.

Within moments of waking, he realized two important facts. First, squint as he might, he couldn't see land; and, he didn't remember getting into the boat. "Must have been some party!" he reasoned.

After awhile his eyes found a short wooden oar. He picked it up and began to row. "Wherever home is," he thought, "it ain't here."

Before an hour had passed, Adam became weary. His muscles ached for liniment; his stomach growled for food; and his heart longed for home.

He had no idea that help was on the way: three coast guard cutters and a disintegrating raft were already en route.

A Behavioral Expert

The first of these four helpers arrived, parting the thick fog like a slowly-pulled stage-curtain, and announced to Adam, with some certainty, that he could help.

"You've got to make some changes in your rowing-behavior there, son, if you plan to make it to, uh, wherever it is you're headed.

"It's the way you are using that oar; it's all wrong. You must tilt it more, like this. You'll find that to be a much more efficient angle. And, you must get more thrust from your legs."

Adam took the behavior-focused-helper at his word. (He would have accepted philosophy from a two year old at that point.) He changed his rowing behavior, and to his surprise, the pain of rowing was immediately reduced.

But, after awhile, Adam realized that he was still lost at sea, and still homesick.

A Thought Master

Another boat arrived. It was skippered by a helper who also was eager to give advice. "If you want relief from your feelings, Adam, you must change the way you are thinking.

"I can see the pain on your face. Pain like that can only be caused by your emotions, and the only way to change those slippery little suckers is to change the thoughts in your head.

"It all starts with telling yourself the truth. Yep, you've got to tell yourself the truth, Adam, not a pack of lies and half-truths. Don't say to yourself, 'I am weak;' say 'I am strong.' Don't say, 'I will never make it home;' say instead, 'I will be home again.' And, for pity's sake, never say, 'I must' or 'I should;' say only 'I can, if I so desire'."

"And," said Adam, "if water splashes me in the face, should I say, 'Isn't this fine dirt for planting corn?'"

"Don't be ridiculous, Adam, that would be a lie. I am saying your thoughts cause your emotions. So, concentrate on thinking true and helpful thoughts. Get rid of those which are untrue and cause you pain. You've got enough trouble there without adding pain-causing thoughts to your cargo."

The veil of fog closed and took the thought-helper from view. But when Adam put his advice into practice, he did find that his words about truth were true. His stinking-thinking had been hindering him from getting a healing-feeling.

He rowed on, with more efficient behaviors and more adaptive thoughts. Time passed.

While Adam worked like a metronome, a couple of problems still lingered. He was lost and he was homesick. It was impossible for him to deny the truth of that.

A Perspective Changer

Eventually, a third helper became visible. This helper was old enough to be the father of the first two. He looked a little more like a retired college professor than the captain of a boat.

"Your problem is quite clear to me, young man. You are in pain, homesick, because you believe some mythical Eden exists on the other side of all this water, and that you have a right to live there. But, Adam, I can save you a lot of trouble, if you will listen carefully.

"There are no Edens to be found. None. There never was one to lose. If you rowed for a thousand years in each of the directions on your compass, including straight down and straight up, you couldn't find a place that doesn't exist."

Adam swallowed his hope. The professor continued. "Don't despair. That's just the bad news. There's good news too. You have great power, the power of human choice. You can choose any attitude, for yourself, in any circumstance you fall into.

"While there is no island of ultimate rest out there, and there is no home for you to return to, you can find a home; you can make your boat the island you are looking for, if that's what you choose."

And with that he was gone, taking with him the last of Adam's ambition.

Adam pulled the oar from the water and laid it across the boat. He sat back and let his body rest, as if it had no bones.

Time passed again, this time leaving Adam with a surprising thought. Perhaps the last advice was the best. There is no pain in my muscles now—I'm not rowing. There are very few thoughts in my head—it seems pointless to put them there. Maybe I can turn this boat into Eden.

Adam and the Hermit

"Oh, I wouldn't count on that!" Adam turned around just in time to see a Huck-Finn-styled raft pass through the mist and ram his boat. THUD!

The impact threw Adam's bottom to the wooden floor of his boat. From there he heard a loud splash and then felt the impact of several gallons of water cascading down on his head.

Adam peered over the side of his boat. He saw nothing. Then, suddenly, two wet hands surfaced and grabbed hold of Adam's boat, inches from his nose. A dripping, wet, beard-encircled head followed and stared at Adam, eye-to-eye.

The stranger seemed undaunted by the collision. And, from the looks of his dirty face, in need of a bath.

The little man hoisted himself from the dark water like a gymnast on a pommel horse. He landed on his feet on the back cross-seat in Adam's boat in such a manner that it caused Adam to wonder if he planned to surf. Then he abruptly sat down, with a loud, wet splat.

"Hello there, Adam," the man said.

A smile pushed at Adam's lips as he gazed at the stranger.

The little man was barefooted and wore what was left of a pair of jeans and a T-shirt. Water dripped from the tips of his curly brown hair and glistened from within the caverns of his beard. His eyes were penetrating beams of light.

The little man returned Adam's unintended smile and asked, "Where were you going at such a molasses-in-January pace?"

"I'm going nowhere," Adam said, "because there is nowhere to go."

"Ah, I see," said the stranger, as a drop of water dove from his nose to the bottom of the boat.

"So," said Adam, "you also know that there is nowhere to go, no Edens for the homesick."

"No," replied the little man.

"No?" said Adam, with a soft ring of hope returning to his voice.

"No," came the quick reply. "I understand that you have probably encountered my friend, the professor, and that now, if that is the case, your head is more content than your heart."

"Then I suppose," said Adam, more than a little sarcastically, "you have brought the gift, the only true wisdom?"

"No," the little man replied, as his eyes continued to sparkle and pop, "for a gift to be truly a gift, it must also be received. I can tell you about a mysterious wisdom. But, only you can turn that into a gift."

"Well," sighed Adam. "I'm about as receptive as a used catcher's mitt; fire away."

Adam and His Leaps Toward Home

"OK then," said the hermit-looking little man. "The first thing you have to do is simple. You've got to die."

Adam swallowed hard and quickly scanned his passenger to make sure he wasn't carrying a weapon, or an unused bottle of anti-psychotic medication."

The hermit continued. You must die to any hope that you

can, in any way, help yourself. Any sense of self-sufficiency, any remaining feelings of self-determination, any stash of willfulness must be thrown overboard. When this is done and the door to your heart is ready to swing inward, well, then you will be fit for the journey."

Adam looked puzzled, but the hermit continued. "Half of your work is already complete. Your oar is already out of the water. You have seen the futility of your own willful efforts.

"But, your letting go must be accompanied by trust, and by hope, not just exhaustion or despair. So, let go and hope. Hope for Eden, hope for compassion, hope for security, hope for the warm embrace of a long-lost father."

Adam closed his eyes for a few seconds, or perhaps it was a few days—it's hard to say when you can't see the sun.

The words he had just heard rose to the top of his head and began to fall like a warm summer rain on the furrows of his soul. The next time he opened his eyes, tender green shoots of willingness were beginning to grow deep within. He gazed out. The fog was melting. The hermit was smiling.

Adam was a little surprised—the hermit was still in the boat. It was then that Adam saw his only unhomely feature—two deep blue eyes which seemed to be bottomless reservoirs of peace.

Sunlight. Adam felt, and saw, sunlight. What earlier would have been an oppressive opponent was now the visual equivalent to Handel's "Hallelujah Chorus." It cascaded through the retreating fog and sparkled over the now blue-green water in patches of diamonds.

He let himself enjoy the sun and the delicate breeze that whispered through his hair as it brought the fresh smell of the ocean. Sea gulls spoke to each other, high overhead. He let out a thousand-dollar sigh.

"That's right, Adam. You have just discovered a wonderful gift—the present moment. You've been a crime victim up until now, you know. Your most precious possession, your only true possessions, had been taken from you—your present moments. But now you have them all back."

It was then that Adam became aware of movement.

He looked at the hermit with a question in his eyes. "Yep, we're moving all right. Now that you have let go of your own efforts, the current that you have been rowing against is taking you back home. Willingness and hope are the keys—not just inactivity—to your rescue. You're going home."

For a long while Adam enjoyed the company of the hermit, and he enjoyed his five new friends, his senses.

Then, just at a particular present moment, an ungodly shriek rang out. It pierced the air like a screaming missile and landed right on Adam's adrenal gland. He whirled in the direction from where the cry had come and found himself staring up into the yellow eyes of a five-story sea monster.

The creature towered over Adam and the hermit. It was at least three times as wide as the boat they sat on. Claws, longer than a man's body, extended from wildly-flailing hands. Its wake turned Adam's boat into a cardboard car on a roller coaster.

Instinctively, Adam spun himself around, grabbed the oar and began to jab the water with all his might. His efforts were futile. The creature was so close that Adam could smell its warm breath.

The sea monster let go of another heart-stopping scream. Adam stole a quick glance at the hermit. He was yawning.

"For the love of God, man, aren't you going to help before we both die!" The little man grinned a broad-toothed grin. "By the love of God, Adam, I thought you were already dead. Didn't we just talk about that? Plus, Adam," the hermit spoke over the high-pitched shrieks of the monster, "no one was ever killed by an illusion. Unless, of course, he was stupid enough to believe the illusion were real."

With his little boat tossed in monster-wake, Adam was quite certain that it was real water which was splashing him in the face.

"Adam," the hermit continued, "the wisdom that says 'let go' does not say 'strive again.' Keep your oar in the boat and stare down this illusion. It's just a projection of your unfounded fears!" The hermit said this as fresh sea water dripped from his chin.

Whether out of blind faith or futility, Adam stopped his rowing once more. In a matter of seconds the sea monster's head was directly over Adam's; it was coiled and ready to strike, like a serpent.

Adam's heart was exploding within his chest like jungle drums, as the monster's scale-encircled mouth came crashing down, encircling Adam.

Adam somehow found the faith he was searching for—"It's not real! It's not real!"—as the monster's mouth passed through him, with less effect than the beam of an X-ray. Instantly, the creature disappeared, like darkness from a suddenly lighted room.

Adam, chest heaving, tongue dry, shot a relieved glance at the hermit. The hermit was eating a sandwich. He smiled at Adam through the bread crumbs on his mouth, and said, "Now this peanut butter sandwich is real. Want some?" Adam slowly shook his head no.

"Well, anyway, you're still headed in the right direction, I see."

Adam collapsed to the bottom of the boat, his heart still beating almost as loud as the hermit's smacking.

When Adam had mustered the energy to sit back up, the hermit spoke. "You're almost home."

"I'm not so sure I want to go any more," said Adam. "Not if monsters like that live there."

"Oh, they don't. Monsters like that live only in your heart. As long as one's heart remains dirty, soiled with doubt, bitterness, fear, or anger, these illusions will be created—in much the same way that shadowy-specks are cast onto a movie screen if the lens of the projector has not been wiped clean."

"You mean," said a very concerned Adam, "this could happen again?"

"Oh, yeah, even after experiencing the peace of surrendering to willingness, many spend the rest of their lives frantically rowing, trying to escape from the illusionary projections, projections caused by light trying to shine through the debris in their own hearts."

"Then how does a heart become clean?"

Before the last word passed through Adam's teeth, he was startled by loud crackling and popping sounds. He turned and saw a fire raging on top of the water. The fire was so high that its flames licked at the bottom of the sky. The immense heat followed closely behind the sounds. It felt like a desert hurricane.

Adam knew that they would be in the eye of the inferno within seconds. He whirled and cried out to his friend, "Is this illusion?! IS THIS ILLUSION?!"

"No," the hermit shouted over the noise of the fire, "This is real, and you must not try to escape it!"

For reasons he did not understand, Adam grabbed his own knees instead of his oars and threw himself into a ball in the bottom of the boat. Within seconds it was engulfed by the towering flames. He screamed a real scream, a shrieking, blood-curdling scream, that was quickly gobbled up by the fire. The pain was very real. The wooden boat crackled in his ears. He smelled his own skin burning. All went black.

When Adam awoke, his body was still tightly curled. He lay on his side, staring at the side of his boat. His head was half-submerged in water.

He sprang to his feet. He inspected the boat. There were no traces of burning. He inspected himself. He seemed whole and without scar. He looked for his friend. But Adam was now alone in the boat. "HEY!!" he shouted. "Where are you?!"

The only sounds that returned were his own echo and the melodious cooing from just over his head.

Adam looked up at a brightly-white dove. It was wearing the late afternoon sun like a halo, and had the hermit's smiling eyes. Adam began to weep. The dove slowly circled Adam's down-turned head, and then, floated away with the gentle sea breeze.

Just before the dove had completely faded from view, and while tears still streamed down Adam's face, the movement of his boat came to an abrupt halt. He had run aground.

Adam picked himself up from his second trip to the bottom of his boat. He turned to gaze, opened-mouthed, at a post-card-perfect picture of nature's sculpture.

His boat had come to rest in the snow-white sand of a broad beach. The beach trimmed a majestic island like lace on an Easter dress. The white of the sand faded into the emerald green of thick, rich tropical plant life, and this green rolled out like plush carpet, up and over gentle slopes. It unfurled at the foot of a range of jagged, deep-purple mountains.

Adam hurled himself from the boat and made face-down snow angels in the sand.

Then, just when Adam thought his heart would burst with joy, a tantalizing aroma began to fill his nose. It was the smell of roasting fish.

Adam sprang to his feet. He stared at a strangely-familiar-looking figure who sat by the fire, less than fifty yards away. The man, oddly-dressed in white and purple, stood and waved at Adam with great eagerness.

Adam swallowed twice to keep his heart inside. He began to walk, and then to run, toward the man.

When he was about twenty yards away, he stopped dead in his tracks. He dug into a pocket and pulled out a twice-bitten apple. He tossed it to an outbound wave and continued on.

The one who stood by the fire opened his arms wide and Adam fell into a warm embrace, as he heard, "Welcome home, my prodigal son. I've been waiting for you."

2

Adam and the Three Unhelpful Helpers

All of us are homesick for Eden.
We yearn to return to a land we've never known.
Deep is the need to go back to the garden,
A burning so strong, for a place we belong,
A place that we know is home.

Paul Smith

Occasionally, I am surprised by an unusual realization. For instance, one day while driving to work it dawned on me that I had spent over eleven years of my life sound asleep. As the scenery sped by, I quickly made further calculations. I discovered that I had spent over four months putting on or taking off clothes, a solid two months brushing my teeth, a week saying good-bye, three days doing nothing but blowing my nose, and at least fifteen minutes jogging (well, definitely ten if you count stretching).

In some of that leftover time, I had gone about some activities that were truly important; like the five months I had spent talking to my wife and the three months playing with my children. I was embarrassed, however, by how little time I had actually given to those last two activities. I had spent almost as much time on plaque removal.

When I ran my job as a clinical psychologist through the

mental calculator, I figured I had spent the equivalent of seventeen months—that's twenty-four hours a day, seven days a week listening to individuals, families, and small groups talk about their lives, their pains, their fears, and their hopes. I felt very privileged, and more than a little undeserving, of this staggering amount of time with which I had been entrusted.

Since coming to these realizations, I have logged a few more "weeks" of counseling. I continue to reflect on the disclosures that take place in the privacy of my counseling office. I think about the incredible diversity of people, the myriad of individual differences, and of individualized pain. There is certainly a sense in which a person's pain is like his or her face; no one possesses an exact copy.

But I also think about what seems to be an amazing unity of experience. I can say with conviction, that when I spend even a single hour with a client, one of three distinct themes will be evidenced. And in multiple sessions all three will emerge. I am presently more astonished by this apparent unity than by the previously mentioned diversity. I refer to these shared themes as "compassion deficits," "behavioral narcotics," and "the two selves." Let's talk about each of them.

Compassion Deficits

If the human psyche is viewed as an elaborate engine, then surely love is the oil that keeps it running smoothly.[1]

When I was a teenager and competing for one of the family cars, my dad used to say in jest, "Remember, son, it's OK to run a car without gas, but you had better not run it without oil." The humor is, of course, that it's OK to run the car without gas because it won't run, and consequently no damage will be done. To run a car without oil is, unfortunately, possible. It won't run far before it's time to air out the credit card and repair the damage.

It seems that the human psyche (mind and emotions) was

designed to run while being bathed with the oil of love. A pro-liferation of studies in the area of mind-body relations calls our attention to the fact that love, hope, and laughter heal, while fear and anger destroy.[2] For some, these findings are not sur-prising and serve as a reminder of the truth that our minds and bodies were designed for an environment we no longer live in—Eden, a place of intimate relationship between Creator and creation, between creation and creation, a place whose name means "delight" or "enjoyment." Unfortunately, for many of us our address has become a lonely and isolated "vale of tears."

It is particularly imperative, during the early, formative years (when the engine is being broken in), to avoid running the human psyche without a full crank case of compassion. I have observed that well-oiled psyches are capable of enormous strain. However, internal "engines" which have been run with only a precious few drops of acceptance and nurture often experience unnecessary wear and tear, occasionally locking down completely.

Without exception, all of the individuals I have seen in counseling quickly led me to times and places in their lives where they had experienced traumatic compassion deficits. Usually, the results are a lifetime of running their "engines" without enough oil, physical and psychological wear-and-tear, and a deep-seated desire to go home where love can be found.

Behavioral Narcotics

Like mechanical engines, the heat and friction within the human psyche caused by being forced to run without enough lubrication produce real, sometimes physical, damage. Unlike mechanical engines, this damage produces pain. Not being loved enough hurts. Receiving rejection when we desperately need the balm of acceptance hurts. Being criticized when we thirst for praise hurts.

It is at this point that the engine metaphor breaks down.

Engines stop, but people, most of the time, keep going. Life continues whether or not we are a couple of quarts low on our most needed psyche-lubricant—compassion.

So, how does one continue on while his innards clank and groan in pain? We search for something to deaden the pain, of course. For some clients with whom I have worked, the "narcotics" they have begun to use are real chemicals illegally used substances or alcohol, which are ingested to provide brief emotional vacations from the painful friction in their lives. With these compounds in their systems, reality is momentarily blurred for these hurting souls.

For many others the "narcotics" are not chemical at all, but rather patterns and habits of behavior, relating, or coping which have been developed for the purpose of easing the emotional pain of compassion deficits. Here are some of those habit patterns.

Habits of workaholism: filling the mind so full of thoughts, dreams, and activities of success that there is little room left to feel pain caused by irrational, underlying feelings of inadequacy.

Habits of control: constantly striving to maintain control of others, making their wills the servants of our own, and binding the hands we secretly fear will strike us.

Habits of people pleasing: constantly monitoring what others expect from us so that we can avoid the pain of their rejection by minimizing its likelihood; becoming in the process slaves of our servanthood.

Habits of dependency: always surrendering our will to the will of another (even to God) for reasons of fear and self-diagnosed inadequacy, instead of enjoying the freedom to follow the advice of love.

Habits of perfectionism: wearing a mask of perfection and rightness to cover inner turmoil and ambiguity.

Habits of escape: taking emotional vacations from pain through the use of alcohol, drugs, or self-destructive patterns of pain-delaying behavior.

These are but a few of the countless patterns of behavior which can become coveted narcotics to dull the ache of compassion deficits. To paraphrase the words of Henri Nouwen, in *Out of Solitude,* in some way or another we often sell our souls to the "raters and grade givers" of the world, hoping that by winning their acceptance or by minimizing the possibility of their rejection, we will ease the pain of the initial insult(s) given to our psyches.

Even when words of praise and acceptance are won, they are like oil dropped on a dangerously hot engine. They don't get to the heart of the real problem and they provide no real relief. But even when we are able to win the highest marks, when we finally win their words of commendation, we are inevitably reminded that our engines still groan from friction, and that we have been driving on a road which was not of our own choosing.

What do we do? We try again. We go back to the behavioral narcotic, because just the process of its use serves as a pain deadener for a little while, blocking our deepest and dullest ache—our homesickness for Eden.

Two People in One Chair

There is a third theme I have observed in the lives of my clients. Sitting in the client's chair, there are always two people and they are battling for occupancy. It's as if a cosmic game of musical chairs is in progress. To use the words of Thomas

Merton, a "false self" and a "true self" are jockeying for the final throne.

Perhaps that needs a little explanation. Jacob Needleman, in his book *Money and the Meaning of Life*,[3] tells from Jewish folklore a legend about King Solomon. The story is no more a historical fact than the story of Pinocchio, but it arguably contains at least a measure of moral and spiritual truth. It certainly helps us understand distinctions between the true and false self.[4]

Needleman's interpretation of the Solomon legend goes like this:

Solomon and the True and False Self

Solomon's task was to build a temple, the place in which the highest Holiness could be contacted. The place he was to build was material and external; but it symbolized a spiritual and internal construction as well.

Solomon discovers, however, that to build the temple he must have a special tool for cutting the huge stones. This special all-penetrating tool will be able to cut through the hardest stone in the world, and through the hardest of human hearts. He discovers to his dismay that the tool is presently in the possession of Asmodeus, chief of demons.

Consulting with his elders, Solomon devises a plan to take the tool from Asmodeus. He sends his most trusted servant to the mountains of darkness, the home of Asmodeus, to trick the demon.

While Asmodeus is away, Solomon's servant puts wine in the well. Asmodeus returns and overcome by thirst, he drinks from the well filled with wine and falls into a stupor.

The servant, armed with chains and a special signet ring (it bears the great seal of Solomon—the six-pointed star), is able to capture the disoriented Asmodeus. He brings him back to the palace of Solomon.

In time, Solomon is able to learn of the whereabouts of the special tool from his captive. He also learns that the tool is called a "shamir," and that it is symbolic of a penetrating force whose actions allow life to flourish where, until its use, no life could grow.

Solomon obtains the "shamir" and completes the temple.

Long afterward, with Asmodeus still in chains, Solomon goes to the place where he is kept. Solomon's insatiable desire for wisdom makes him vulnerable; he wants to learn, even from the chief of demons.

"Tell me," says Solomon to Asmodeus, "what is the nature of your power? How is it that you rule so mightily over mankind?"

With that opening, Asmodeus devises a plan to trick Solomon.

He tells him that he will share that secret with him, but Solomon must first unbind him and let him hold the signet ring of the king—the symbol of his true identity.

Solomon takes the risk. He unbinds Asmodeus and hands him the sacred ring.

In a lightning flash, Asmodeus swells to enormous size. The bottom of his wings touch the earth; the tops extend into the highest realms of the heavens. In an instant Asmodeus swallows Solomon and hurls him (literally) with such force that he lands far away from holy Jerusalem—the city of God—far away from the temple. He is in a distant and alien country.

Asmodeus throws the ring into the vast darkness of the ocean. With Solomon dripping wet and the sacred ring in the depths of the sea, Asmodeus enters the inner chambers of the king. He puts on the royal garments, including the king's crown, and then changes his face into the face of Solomon. Asmodeus sits on the throne in place of the real king. His transformation is so convincing that no one knows that it is now Asmodeus, not Solomon, who rules over them.

The secret of Asmodeus' power over men is now seen.

And this is the secret: the power of Asmodeus is his ability to take on the face and the function of the true ruler—the true self within! The power of all the other demons derives from this chief power of Asmodeus. The chief weakness of man is his false sense of *I*. The true king is in exile! A usurper has taken the throne![5]

The legend continues. Solomon, now in a similar socio-economic class as the prodigal son during the time he spent in the pigpen, tries to make a new life for himself.

Solomon's clothes slowly turn to rags as he lives the life of the poorest beggar. He wanders the countryside crying out, "I am Solomon! I was king of Jerusalem!" He is treated as if he were a madman. He becomes a target for insults and stones. Solomon is brought low in every respect. He experiences his nothingness apart from his true identity.

Asmodeus, ruling in Solomon's place, committed many excesses; yet the subjects of the kingdom never assumed that their king was anyone but Solomon. The kingdom, under Asmodeus, came to resemble the devastated lands in *The Lion King*, after the wicked "Scar" was ruling in place of "Simba."

Things improve for Solomon. He falls in love with a woman who, incredibly, returns his love. One day while fishing to keep them both alive, Solomon catches a large fish. He is proud of his catch and brings it home to his wife. But when it is cut open for cleaning, his signet ring falls to the ground.

Solomon picks up the ring and places it on his finger. He stands tall and radiates his former majesty. Though dressed as a beggar, he *is* King Solomon. His wife recognizes the miracle and insists that he make the journey back to Jerusalem to assume his throne. He does, with her at his side.

In the last scene of the legend King Solomon, wearing rags, walks into the palace and confronts Asmodeus, who looks more like Solomon than Solomon himself. There is no cosmic conflict, no Luke Skywalker-Darth Vader lightsaber fight. The true king (the true self within), meets eye-to-eye with the false king (the false self who rules over the impulses of our fallen nature).

Slowly Solomon raises his hand and shows Asmodeus the sacred ring. Asmodeus vanishes in an instant, vacating the throne for the true king. The true self sits on the throne and prosperity returns to the kingdom.

I have heard no more compelling telling of what blocks man from enjoyment of the kingdom of God than this. A false sense of "I" (with no appreciation for "we") rules us from the throne of our hearts.

In my work with clients, I have become aware of the pain of "compassion deficits," the temptation to ease this pain through the use of "behavioral narcotics," and the fact that there are two kings—one true and one false, who vie for the throne of each life.

The false self, the usurper, wants to maintain control at all costs. If it feels the pain of a compassion deficit, it offers a simple solution—find a better "narcotic," but maintain control at all costs.

The true self, the exiled Solomon, wants more. It wants to restore the rightful order and to assume its proper identity. When the true self reigns, love is king in the place of fear, anger, complacency, and narcissism. Its rightful reign is the only true solution to compassion deficits and the substance abuse problem of behavioral narcotics.

When the false self rules, our lives will eventually resemble the devastated wastelands produced by the rule of "Scar" and "Asmodeus."

But we still have a problem. How does the true self find its way back home?

In chapter one the journey of Adam is presented as a parallel to that of King Solomon. It is a journey from wastelands to promised land.

The legend didn't tell us much about Solomon's return trip. But the old hermit guided "Adam" through the "eight giant leaps" he needed to make in order to return home.

Adam and His Rowing

In this story "Adam" is every person. He represents the Adam of the Garden, and as such is a representative of us all. The Adam of the boat is also a composite of the majority of clients I have worked with as a counselor. The three common themes I find in counseling (compassion deficits, behavior narcotics, and the battle between the true and false self for control of the will) are also present in Adam.

Adam suffers the pain of a compassion deficit. In his case it is not acid scars on his heart caused by the careless slinging of criticism from an unthinking parent. Neither is his pain caused by someone who sought his own perverse gratification through emotional or sexual exploitation. It is not even caused by the hurt of unrequited love—giving love to another who cannot return it, because something else (drugs, alcohol, or a career) is his mistress.

Adam's compassion deficit is similar to all of the above. Indeed, it is identical in its effect—pain. His lost-love pain is the grandparent of all compassion deficits. It is separation from the Supreme Lover. It is separation from relationship with God. It is the separation which makes all people subject to the feelings of compassion deficit.

The activity of rowing is used to symbolize a reliance on behavioral narcotics. For some of us Adams, the tenacious rowing process is a striving for accomplishments and trophies that we hope will substitute for the wonderful feelings of life in the paradise that we have lost. The next promotion, the next pay increase, a house overlooking the fairway, the power to impose our will on those with whom we work; these may become our goals—the powerful pain-deadening narcotic of choice.

Rowing, striving, burning the midnight oil and next week's adrenaline; this is the "rowing" process. But as Adam continues to row—to stick the needle into already scarred veins—he realizes that the effect of the narcotic diminishes each time it is released into his lifeblood.

As Dallas Willard puts it: "The true effect of the Fall was to lead us to trust in the flesh alone ... because we now suppose (like mother Eve) that, since there is no God to be counted on in the living of our lives, we must take things into our own hands."[6] This process may spiral downward. We feel the pain of living without the healing balm of divine love; yet we place our trust in the tangible—ourselves—to provide the relief from our suffering.

It is as if we were living in a biosphere on the moon and we decided to go for a walk outside the protective, life-supporting dome. We step out into the oxygen-less atmosphere and begin to gasp for air. But then because our trust is in ourselves, we head out into the wilderness in search of air to breathe instead of turning around and walking back inside to the safety of the dome. We run wildly, we row frantically, to find relief—trusting our oxygen-starved muscles for our salvation instead of returning to safety.

Adam shares the third theme that ties him to all mankind. He is not one, but two. He has two kings buried deeply in his heart. They vie for power in a cosmic struggle between good and evil, which is the subject of all classic fairy tales.

Cigarette smoke drifted across the small country restaurant in slowly expanding curls. The smell of frying bacon was fanned out from the kitchen by a saloon-styled swinging door, which was kept in perpetual motion by two hurried waitresses. The fat-laden fragrance tempted me to ignore my battle with cholesterol. The aroma was so thick I was undoubtedly getting a harmful measure of secondary cholesterol anyway. I reasoned I might as well have the pleasure.

But my attention was directed away from my stomach, first to the backs of my legs, that in the August heat had become one with the yellow, vinyl-covered bench I was sitting on, and second to the voice of my companion who talked on and on, unaware of my lapse of attention. He talked on across half-full cups of coffee and plates that were stained bright yellow by the remnants of our breakfast. He looked out of place in this setting. Not "mink coat at a swimming pool" out of place, but definitely "alligator shoes at a county fair" out of place.

His speech was free of accent and had a smooth FM quality. His tie, which was the only one present in a sea of overalls, was made of silk. I would have bet the price of my breakfast that his suit left little change from a five hundred dollar bill, and the sunlight revealed something rarely seen on a man in those parts—the glint of hair spray.

I'm not making fun—although a few good ole boys did give him a second and a third look. I was pleased to be seen with this gentleman. After all, he was a nationally known consultant; a trouble shooter par excellence who was paid handsomely to tell pastors how to better administer, lead, and shepherd their congregations. He was good. As best as I could tell, his biggest problem was convincing his well-pleased customers not to worship him.

But I was wrong about that. He set his coffee cup back inside the saucer, cleared his throat, and asked me if I minded if he changed topics. I nodded ... he talked. He talked for more than two hours. The restaurant emptied and refilled with lunch customers. When he finished, I knew that his biggest problem was not how to avoid being viewed as a prophet.

During the course of his soliloquy, I had been transported back across decades of time. Instinctively, he had used his visual and poetic gifts to create a vivid picture of the path that led from his early childhood to the small country restaurant that now surrounded us.

He had grown up in a strict, religious environment. He had been introduced to the surrounding world by an emotionally cold, domineering mother (who viewed life with jaundiced eyes) and by a loving, but seldom available, workaholic father. From his earliest memory, his heart belonged to "daddy." While he sensed this may have bothered his mother, she was generally nonplused by the loss of her son's heart. After all, she had the bigger prize—his fertile mind.

My friend was often told by both his parents that he was a "child of destiny," a "special gift from God." He had been born after his mother's biological clock had struck midnight, or so she had thought. This "destiny" was a blessing and a curse. He was blessed with the full focus of family attention (at least when his father was home). He was cursed by the weight of an unwanted mantle. Somehow, he was to be another Moses, or St. Francis, or Martin Luther King, Jr. He was to set his people free ... to point the way to a promised land.

He felt the oppressive weight of that responsibility at the early age of five. The expectations were enormous. He was to live a life free from sin. He was to be perfect. He was to accept the role of messiah (thank goodness with only a little "m"), and all of the preparations which were part and parcel of that calling.

Blessed with a keen intellect, he excelled in his academic preparations. Blessed with a strong will and a Patriot missile-like conscience, he had been able to shoot down, or so he had thought, most assaults to his pharisaic religiosity.

As a teenager he was an A+ student with an award-spangled athletic sweater, and he had a chain of perfect attendance Sunday school pins so long that a lesser athlete might trip on it on the way to the altar. He had everything—a loving father and a doting, omnipresent mother. He had the admiration of his teachers and the respect of his peers, who annually put him in the role of their leader. He had everything that could be hoped for (and more), except for one thing. He didn't have the assurance that he was loved and accepted just for being himself, even *if* he never became a world leader.

A dry and barren part of his soul longed for the cool, steady showers of unconditional love. The boy who looked to the world to have it all, grew up to be a man who was still missing what was most important. That man who sat across from me, still appearing to have everything, felt as if he had nothing. He felt the searing pains of a fifty-year-old compassion deficit.

He spoke openly of this pain and of his attempts at self-treatment through the use of behavioral narcotics (striving, running, rowing, in search of Eden). His life was now at a time of crisis. He recognized that his pursuit to attain "trophies" was analogous to the use of "narcotics" to ease pain—in his case, the pain of not feeling genuinely and unconditionally loved.

The dreams his mother had imposed on him, and the accepted goals he had chosen for himself, were poured from the same vial. The knowledge that he was using a behavioral narcotic lessened its effect even more; an effect already weakened through the "tolerance" that was building up in his system. Something had to change. He had to find his way out of Plato's cave, back to Eden.

The First Helper

The first three helpers Adam encountered were psychologists, but they were not "soul-ologists." There are very few of those today. They were behavioral, cognitive, and world-view engineers, in that order.

The first helper was a behaviorist. As a science, behaviorism is as new as the late nineteenth-century laboratory of Ivan Pavlov. As a practice, it is older than St. Gregory's emphasis on regular and consistent positive reinforcement of desired behaviors for his monastic followers in the sixth century.[7] Perhaps as old as the punishment of Adam and Eve.

I was first exposed to behavioral psychology in the mid-70s. I was an undergraduate psychology major at a major university in the south. It was at the height of the halcyon days of behaviorism. Rats were being taught how to play ping pong and pigeons how to play shuffleboard. (They weren't that good at it, however—the graduate students won most of the games.)

The behaviorists had taken over the psychology department, except for two humanistic-oriented professors, who were closer than they knew to retirement. That environment was very shaping for me. I proudly became a card-carrying member of the behavioral school of thought.

After graduation, however, I began to slowly drift away from a sold-out behavioral position. Exposure to other schools of psychological thought, not to mention client resistance to my charts and graphs, and the embarrassment of "symptom substitution" (that humiliating situation in which you help a client correct one problem behavior, only to have two new ones crop up elsewhere), were precipitating factors in my drifting process.

I am still proud of my behavioral training and rely on it often when working with clients. I still consider myself a card-carrying behaviorist—although it is a bit tattered, surrounded by many other cards, and covered with wallet goo. The students I teach hear me say ad nauseam, "As long as people can only do three things (think, feel, and behave) they will need to learn ways to help them do those three things better."

Clearly, one of the things we don't do well is behave. It follows that people helpers should possess skills in the area of facilitating behavioral change. I am also convinced that many of our problem behaviors are in reality outgrowths of other problems. They are the result of our attempts to relieve the unbearable tension resulting from our failure in dealing with the disappointment of our deepest longings for love and relationship.[8]

In its most radical form, behaviorism may miss this message. Radical behaviorism is loosely represented by Adam's first helper. What he offers is advice that ignores the existence of the mind. It avoids giving attention to conscious processes. It assumes that the only valid subject matter in psychology is observable behavior. That's great for helping someone behave in a less painful manner. However, Adam's "compassion deficit" is ignored by the first helper. His being lost and away from "home" is also ignored. It's irrelevant. It means nothing to the first helper. But these factors are not inconsequential to Adam. He needs love. He needs reconciliation. He needs to fall back into the arms of a Father who has been waiting for his return. For Adam to simply "row" more efficiently and with less physical pain is not, ultimately, helpful. Indeed, it takes him further away from the solution to his dilemma. It is almost as bad as prescribing a time management workshop for a workaholic. Wait a minute. It's exactly that bad!

The Second Helper

Adam is offered advice from a second helper who tells him that his thoughts, more than his behavior, are the fundamental problem. This helper represents a second dominant school of psychology—cognitive psychology.

Cognitive and cognitive-behavioral therapies have become enormously popular during the past two decades. While cognitive psychology historically may not be one of the top three on the list, it is definitely on the chart and rising like a rocket. It also directly addresses the second of the three things humans can and must do—think.

The word cognitive, of course, refers to an individual's thoughts. The techniques of cognitive therapy are complex and require supervision to master. The theory, however, is very simple. Just as a jukebox contains a number of records that can be played when money is dropped into the coin slot and the right buttons are pushed, our minds, so the theory goes, contain a number of records (automatic thoughts) which will play if the right buttons are pushed; the right buttons being a recalling of the circumstances we were in that preceded the thought. And, just as "Your Cheatin' Heart" may produce feelings of sadness and Handel's *Messiah* may cause great exhilaration, our thoughts, caused to play by the events of our day, may subsequently produce a wide range of emotions. It is less the event, and more our stored thoughts, which produce our resulting emotions. The thought-helper would say that if Adam is feeling the wrong feelings, he is thinking the wrong thoughts. This is good because thoughts are easy to change.

I have great respect for the advice of this helper. There does appear to be substantial evidence that our thoughts have a great impact on our emotions. Also cognitive therapies have been shown to be consistently effective for a variety of "feeling problems." Even if this hard data did not exist, I would still be a believer, for I have observed an unmistakable relationship between the songs in *my* head and the feelings in *my* heart.

Cognitive psychotherapy has been readily adopted by many in the Christian environment. Arguably, the cognitive approach has enjoyed more acceptance in Christian circles than any other school of thought imported from psychology. Perhaps cognitive psychology is accepted by Christians because of its central notion that a person's thinking determines his mental health. This idea is consistent with Christian theology (See Philippians 4:4-9, 11, 13).[9]

The advice of the thought-helper was very helpful—as was that of the behavior-helper—toward easing Adam's pain. Adam was, in part, driven by his thoughts. The second helper, like the first, was only minimally interested in exploring the role of compassion deficits in Adam's dilemma. He would become concerned if any of Adam's present maladaptive thoughts could be traced to a *particular* compassion injury. Then, the helper's focus would likely be on correcting Adam's illogical thinking and not upon his need for relationship.

The thought-helper would also be unconcerned as to whether Adam's frantic rowing might have spiritual overtones. He would not worry that it might be a behavioral narcotic. He avoids true and false self issues in favor of true and false thinking concerns.

Make no mistake about it, he gives Adam good advice and Adam is helped. But he is still left with many unanswered questions, such as: "I know these records are playing, but who put them in my jukebox in the first place?"; "Why do I keep playing the same old record when I know it makes me cry?"; and, "Will I ever have someone to dance with?"

The Third Helper

My oldest daughter's favorite movie is *The Princess Bride*. I am sure she has watched it twenty times—last month. In one of my favorite lines, Wesley, the principal hero, following a long time of painful separation from the heroine, announces to her, "Princess, life is hard, and anyone who tells you differently is trying to sell you something."

His statement calls to mind Rabbi Kushner's words in his classic, *When Bad Things Happen to Good People*,[10] "Pain is the price we pay for being alive," and the quote by who knows whom, "Life is short, and then you die."

Occasionally, I find myself in a frame of mind that enjoys contemplating the poignant pessimism which underlies those two phrases. It's an unusual type of enjoyment.

It feels like the simultaneous awareness of excruciating physical pain caused by a blow to the nose, and the ego-pride that comes from having stood your ground with the school bully. Or, perhaps it's more like the merry-melancholy that comes when we are staring out the window at a third consecutive day of drizzling rain and realizing that life will go on, even without a perfect vacation. It feels mature—really mature—to say with the existentialists, "Death, isolation, meaninglessness, these are the givens of human existence. Bring 'em on; I can handle it!"

The third helper arrives as a seasoned sojourner. He brings wisdom. As a representative of a third dominant school of psychological thought—existential psychology, he is not concerned with Adam's inefficient rowing behavior, or his "stinking thinking." This helper's focus is upon the third thing humans can do: feel; and the power they have over their feelings.

He sees Adam as rising above his behaviors and thoughts, superseding the sum of his parts. He tells Adam that his desire for Eden, while understandable, is immature—a childlike fantasy for escaping the pain which is as an inevitable part of living, living that includes rainy days, punctured tires, and letters from the IRS.

The existential-helper believes that Adam's rowing is just a naive means of perpetuating what Heidegger[11] would call an unhealthy "state of forgetfulness." He would say that it serves no purpose but to distract Adam's attention from a healthier awareness. He advises Adam to abandon his escape fantasies, accept the pains and disappointments of existence, including the freedom and the responsibility of his power to choose.

The essence of the third prescription is that Adam should begin with a commitment to himself. Then he will find the meaning he searches for. Adam should trust only himself as he reaches for his destiny. In essence, Adam is told that it is he, himself, who is the ultimate reference point. It is not some mythical place or deity.

To fully accept this advice would be to finish eating the apple from the Garden of Eden, or to lay more bricks on the Tower of Babel. In momentarily accepting it, Adam, like his namesake, is once again cut off from the very source of life. He has made himself the captain of his fate. The advice ("let go") which is the closest to spiritual wisdom, is, in the mouth of the third helper, the farthest from it.

The third helper's wisdom does not address Adam's need to fall into the arms of love. It takes away his behavioral narcotic without working to bring about a healing of the underlying pain that cries out. The soft, quiet voice of Adam's true self is drowned out completely by the boisterous and empowered voice of his false self. At one level Adam is helped more by the third helper than by either of the other two. He has stopped rowing so there is no physical pain. He has minimal thought pain. Adam has been helped, but he has been helped at the expense of true help. Yes, he is captain of his fate, but now he drifts without hope on a meaningless sea.

Years had passed since I last saw my friend, the consultant. All of the good intentions of staying in touch had not produced a single letter from either of us.

My bustling private practice in clinical psychology had occupied the lion's share of my time. I had discovered that the phrase "quality time with the kids" failed to alleviate my guilt, as I battled to spend enough quantity time with them.

My workaholism, my job as a wounded healer, and almost every client I had, caused me to replay some of the past conversations I previously had with my friend. I often wondered about the outcome of his confessed compassion deficit, his private war against behavioral narcotics, and just which of his two selves was getting the most time on the throne in his internal palace.

Then one bright, cold November day I bumped into him. I mean I literally bumped into him, as in "Oh, excuse me for knocking that tray out of your hand. Oh my goodness, I can't believe it's you. What are you doing on this side of the country? May I sit down?"

His face showed no signs of the time that had passed. After a polite, "How have you been?" we got down to the real question, the "How have you really been?" I was delighted to realize that we had maintained the type of relationship where being open and transparent is as easy and natural as breathing.

He quickly launched into the update that I had wondered about. "I've been in therapy," he said.

"Oh," I said attempting an inflection of surprise. "How has that been for you?" I tried hard not to sound like a counselor. Two hours passed in what seemed to be just a moment. My fascination with his story chased time along.

When he finished his story, I decided that he had found a highly competent therapist. His counselor had spotted the workaholism only minutes into the intake interview. The impact of his somewhat unusual relationship with his parents, particularly his enmeshment with his mother, was the topic of dozens of sessions. An intricate pattern of bridges, resembling a "spaghetti junction" where several interstates meet, had been built between his present-day feelings and expectations and his past. He was frequently reminded by his therapist, that while a fifty-plus-year-old man stares back from the bathroom mirror, there is a five-year-old boy looking back at you, too. And he is the one doing most of the feeling.

My friend had also been taught how to row better. He had learned how to strive for happiness (Eden) without feeling so much pain. This took the form of time-management training and encouragement to practice pleasant behavior as a part of each day's routine.

He was taught about the powerful role of thoughts as pre-cursors to emotion. He learned to identify oft-played records—injunctions from his parents such as, "You should be able to do what others cannot," and "You're stupid if you make a mistake," and he learned how to smash them. Then he learned how to cut new, truthful hits.

The wisdom of the third helper was invoked to remind my friend that life is short, too short to be collecting trophies, honors, and awards intended for a grand exchange for happiness. He was encouraged to exercise choice, and to make sure that the choices were his own.

Five minutes before he had to race off to give another packed-house presentation, I fumbled for the obvious question. "So, how do you feel now?" He dropped his eyes and gave himself an uncharacteristically long time for thought. "I feel better, a lot better," he finally replied. "I've put some distance between me and my emotions. I understand them better, and I've even got some control of them."

"So," I said, "you're glad you went in for some counseling?"

"I wouldn't take anything for what I have learned," he said, quite somberly.

"Then, why so glum, chum?" I quipped in my best Yogi Bear voice.

"Because, I still feel empty inside. I still feel more driven to cure than to care. When I'm totally honest with myself, I know that I still reside in a house of fear, instead of a house of love. I have diagnosis, I have insight, but my treatment is only at the surface level. Deep down inside, things still are pretty rotten. You know what diagnosis and insight without real cure is, don't you?"

Yeah, I knew. After all, I was a psychologist and an amateur theologian.

Diagnosis without cure is what is found in hell.

3

The Hermit and the Eight Giant Leaps

When God is centered in us, and we in Him,
we have a home within the true self,
or center, out of which to live.

Leanne Payne
Healing Presence

While I was conducting a seminar on the "emotional hazards of ministry," a pastor told a small group of his peers: "You know, the biggest stress I have, is being asked to be an IBM-styled executive in God's kingdom. It's impossible. The two value systems are at war with each other."

Bobbing heads all around the room let me know that he was not alone in his feelings. For more than an hour, each pastor talked about the personal torque he felt as a result of constantly being pulled in opposite directions.

To be a success in the eyes of many in their congregations, not to mention many of their overseers, these pastors felt that they must produce "bigger and better" products and programs; to stay true to their beliefs about God's kingdom, however, they needed to be seeking after different, and often mutually exclusive, goals.

One pastor summarized the dilemma this way, "There is a loud voice from outside that says, 'to be rewarded you must produce nickels and noses for the kingdom.'" He confessed that he was even told by one supervisor, "Just keep your nose clean, son, and the big churches and big salaries will be yours before you know it."

"But," he went on, "there is a soft internal voice that says, 'My interest is in the purity of my people's hearts.'"

Quite a disturbing dilemma. God's shepherds pulled apart by "Cave" and "kingdom." I wonder what Jesus would say.

Jesus Wasn't Very Flashy

Flashy is not the first adjective which generally comes to mind in describing Jesus, the Servant-King. From his birth when he was laid in manger straw to his burial when he was laid in a borrowed tomb; from his teaching on the blessedness of being ungrudgingly humble and poor to his "coronation" on the back of a donkey; he modeled a value system that was very hard for us cave-dwellers to understand. He is king. But his kingdom is invisible, upside-down, and outside "the cave."

The hermit in the story is a representative of this upside-down kingdom. His casual grooming, neglected clothing, his advice, and the rubble of a raft he rode, all set him apart from the first three helpers Adam encountered. And perhaps he reminds us a little of the desert fathers of early church history.

Adam's frantic rowing (his behavior) is not the point of focus for the hermit. Instead, he peers into the depths of Adam's soul. For the fourth helper, everything but that inward look is blurred at the periphery of his vision. The hermit is a flesh-and-blood representative of the Holy Spirit of God. His focus is more spiritual in scope—walking Adam to the mouth of Plato's Cave—than traditional psychotherapy—advising him about the appropriate ways to behave, think, and feel. Because of divine insight, the hermit knows that Adam's real need is for a healing love that can only be found in the presence of the Supreme Lover. He offers Adam himself. He offers him spiritual wisdom. He directly and indirectly introduces him to the Eight Giant Leaps necessary to get to Eden.

Leap One: Belief that the Kingdom Really Exists

There is a story that has tumbled down from the Appalachian mountains about a boy and his fish. On a particular hot August afternoon the boy was fishing at his favorite fishin' hole, and "catching-em" as fast as he could stab the worms and throw the line back in the water. He wondered if the fish were actually cooperating. Maybe they thought it might be cooler out of the water.

He was yanking them out of the water so fast he didn't have time to string them up. He just pulled the hook out and threw them up on the bank. Well, when his arms got tired, he started gathering up the fish into a big burlap sack. He was surprised to see that one of the first he had caught (he recognized it by an unusual spot on its fish-forehead) was still alive, still "a flappin'." The boy didn't take the time to give it a second thought. He just marched on home, proud as a dog who had caught a stick before it hit the ground.

When he got back home, he decided to leave the cleaning until next morning, and when morning came, he was surprised to see that one of the fish—the one with the spot—was still alive. He cleaned the other fish, but put that one in water. He decided to see if he could teach it to breathe air.

For the next week he worked with the fish. Each day he would leave it out of water for longer periods of time. Eventually, the fish learned how to stay out of water altogether.

That ole fish would follow the boy everywhere he went. He even learned how to roll-over and fetch sticks (small ones, of course). The boy named him Homer. Homer turned out to be the best pet the boy had ever had.

Then when school began in the fall, the boy gathered his school supplies, put his shoes back on, and headed down the road to school. He got halfway there when he heard a strange noise—a slapping, flapping, fish-fin-on-dirt-road, sorta sound. He turned around and saw Homer following him to school.

The boy yelled at his fish to go back, but Homer didn't listen. He stomped one foot at the fish, then the other, and then both at the same time. But Homer just stomped his fin back at the boy and stayed put. Finally, the boy started throwing rocks at Homer, and the fish retreated a few fin-steps. The boy continued on to school.

All was quiet for a while, until the boy was crossing a wooden bridge. Then, he heard it again, that slapping, flapping noise. He ignored it and finished crossing the bridge. Just as he reached the other side, he heard a loud cracking sound. Turning and looking back, he expected to see the fish flopping across the bridge, but there was no Homer. The boy retraced his steps over the bridge. When he got to the middle, he looked down and saw a broken plank. And as he looked down through the hole, he saw Homer down in the water ... drowned.[1]

The story of the boy and the fish reminds me of us and the kingdom of God. Most of us have become so accustomed to life in the Cave—our unnatural environment—that we would probably "drown" if we were suddenly thrust into the kingdom—our natural habitat. But the first of the Eight Giant Leaps home is belief in the kingdom. This is a belief that says the kingdom is truly real and that living there is a possibility—not just in the sweet by and by, but also in the nasty here and now.

While trying the kingdom on for size might be the spiritual equivalent of having an ocean of cold water thrown in your face, we cannot deny that our here-and-now entry into it is the central theme of Scripture. It is the key to understanding the message of Christ.

The Kingdom in Scripture: Not a Fish Story

Jesus begins his brief ministry on earth with the proclamation, "This is the time of fulfillment. The kingdom of God is at hand. Repent and believe the gospel" (Mark 1:15). And he tells us in Matthew (6:33) that entering into the kingdom should be the supreme object of a person's striving. Its entry should be sought above all else. Eleven of the parables of Jesus are introduced with the phrase, "The kingdom is like … " and "the kingdom" is referred to eighty times in the Gospels.

John Bright, a distinguished Old Testament scholar, summarizes his award-winning book, *The Kingdom of God*, with the statement, "The central theme in Scripture is salvation to life in the kingdom."[2] He goes on to state that the concept of the kingdom is the "total message" of the gospel. For him, to understand the kingdom is to understand salvation. To misunderstand the kingdom is to misunderstand salvation.

John Bright offers another chilling observation. While he believes that the kingdom is the central theme of Scripture, and that a common understanding in Old Testament times about the kingdom involved the expectancy of recovering the lost Eden, he points out that the kingdom was missed by the people of that day. The prophets had to use about as much papyrus in pointing out to the people that they had missed the kingdom as Moses had to use in pointing the way *to* the kingdom.

Dallas Willard in a teaching series on the kingdom of God states that the kingdom is still very easy to miss. Yet, he offers, "The reality of the kingdom is the reality of the gospel. Jesus was the reality and the availability of the kingdom."[3] Also, according to Willard, Jesus did only three things while on earth: he announced the kingdom; he taught about its nature; and he demonstrated his authority to do such teaching by performing signs and wonders.

I don't think it is going way out on a limb to say that the first leap in our journey back home to Eden is to believe, really believe, that the kingdom is real, and that we are invited to live within its walls. It is this belief, existing in Adam's heart as a deep longing, a homesickness, that is the first step of turning toward home, and it is the backdrop for the playing out of the next seven steps. Adam wants to go home, even if going there will leave him feeling like a fish, back in water.

Leap Two: Practicing the Presence of God

The hermit apparently feels no need to maintain appropriate professional distance. He climbs right on board with Adam. And in doing so, he becomes an in-the-flesh giver of empathy and understanding. He, too, experiences the discomfort caused by sitting on the hard-plank seats of Adam's boat, to feeling the tickle in his stomach caused by riding the roller coaster of ocean waves. He feels *with* Adam. He feels *what* Adam feels. He is *with* him in the boat and *with* him in his predicament. And because he is there, he allows Adam to practice a healing presence.

God is a god of relationship. He took daily walks with his created children in the Garden of Eden—until they decided to leave home. He had a room built for himself in the Temple in Jerusalem (a God-in-law suite, if you will) and he had another built for himself in the heart of each of us.

He even went so far as to have his Son declare that two supreme commandments were being in a head-over-heels-loving relationship with God, and being in a head-over-heels-loving relationship with each other. And after his Boy was put to death by a bunch of blurry-eyed cave dwellers, he sent another part of himself to stay with us and keep us company. He sent the Holy Spirit.

It would seem that God is pretty heavily into loving relationships. He has done everything possible so that his creation can live in the presence of what they need most—love. It is not surprising, then, that spiritual directors talk so much about the benefits of living in the presence of God. It *is* surprising, however, when so few pilgrims decide to take the leap and live in a moment-by-moment awareness of his presence. And that's a shame, for living in the presence of Love would seem to be *the* most logical treatment plan for those experiencing a compassion-deficit disorder.

Leap Three: Conversing with God

The computer makes us fantastically more able
to calculate and analyze. It does not help us
to meditate.

We have instruments to enable us to see
everything from the nebulae to the neutron—
everything except ourselves.

We have immeasurably extended our gift of sight
but not of insight.

For that, we have the same equipment as the
eighth-century prophets.

Potentially the same, but actually poorer,
for while we have been so busy extending one
aspect of the knowing of telling self, we
have allowed other aspects to atrophy.

We have built ourselves up into power
transmitting stations, but as receiving sets
we are feeble.[4]

John V. Taylor

The "present" hermit and Adam enter into fellowship. They talk. Christians serve a God who says that his precious "sheep" must learn to know his voice. They must be able to distinguish between his voice and that of a "thief" and "robber" if they are to be saved and to enjoy life in full (John 10:1-10). Learning to know his voice is a skill that takes considerable practice to develop.

He further defines himself as the Good Shepherd (verse 11) who willingly lays down his life for the sheep. We also know from Scripture (1 John 1:1-4) that it is the desire of the Good Shepherd, our heavenly Father, to have fellowship with us. And fellowship, according to that great word-ologist, Webster, means friendly companionship, and a mutual sharing of experience, activity, and interest.

John, in his Gospel and first letter, gives the picture of a Shepherd-Daddy who wants his creation to learn his voice through the practice of intimate fellowship and communication. God has wired us with the necessary hardware to receive such communication. With practice we can learn to tune out transmissions from the thief, Satan, and tune in WGOD—a station that features the availability of a twenty-four-hour-a-day counselor—a counselor who dares to discipline but is more likely to love. We can listen to someone who has felt our pain, and *who knows the way home.*

Adam listened to the counselor, and what he heard and obeyed brought him to leap number four—a giant leap!

Leap Four: Embracing Willingness

There is a spiritual longing that hovers around the edges of daily awareness, spiritual experiences and momentary recollections of the "home" that existed before self-definition and independent identity were established. The longing for re-union with this "home" is marginally available to awareness but most of the time we are so preoccupied with other issues that we fail to notice it.[5]

Gerald May, *Will and Spirit*

It appears that the most crucial contrast in all of Scripture is the distinction drawn between willfulness and willingness. Even prior to the first push of a "pen" across a piece of papyrus to write, "In the beginning," Satan had already fallen from grace because he chose willfulness (an attempt to seize power, to be as God) over choosing to surrender to the will of his Creator.

The fundamental choice given to Father Adam and Mother Eve was a choice between eating from the Tree of Life (a choice for willingness) and the Tree of the Knowledge of Good and Evil (a continuation of the willful choice Satan made to be as God). The life of virtually every patriarch can be viewed as a parable of God's faithful reward for the choice of willingness and his punishment for the choice of willfulness.

Jesus taught often using sheep as a model of willingness and goats as a model of willfulness. He contrasted the sheep's gentle compliant character with that of the willful behavior of goats. But Jesus did more than just talk about willingness. He also offered his life as an example of willingness for his followers to emulate (Phil 2:5-11).

It is no coincidence that the church has prized devotional literature which begin with a declaration of willingness. For example, "The Lord is my shepherd ... " and, "Our Father who art in heaven ... thy will be done." It is also interesting to note that the most fundamental and accepted creed of the Christian faith, about the only one upon which all Christian bodies can agree reads, "Jesus is Lord."

As Christians we are members of a club whose membership

dues are extraordinarily high. They call for a profession of the willing statements: "Jesus is the Lord of my life—I am not"; and, "Your kingdom come and, my kingdom go." Gerald May offers the following definition for this level of willingness. "It is the surrender to a reality greater than oneself and relinquishment of the idea that a person can actually master life. We, in essence, surrender our separateness, and say yes to the mystery of being alive in each moment."[6]

Whew! No wonder it is so tempting to try to get in on the club parties without actually paying those hefty dues. By contrast, he defines willfulness as "the setting apart of oneself from the deepest reality in an attempt to master one's own destiny and control and manipulate existence"—you know, false-self stuff.

The theology of the hermit is simple and is built on the fulcrum where willingness and willfulness teeter in our hearts. The hermit believes that Father Adam fell by choosing willfulness over willingness. Father Adam believed Satan's lie which said that more fulfillment was available if he would take matters into his own hands. And he lost Eden.

Adam—the Adam of the boat—must do something about his father's fall. He must get up! The way he gets up is by becoming willing to receive the gift of faith which makes it possible for him to become willing. The hermit invites Adam to choose this new course with a sense of grace-given hope. Adam does as the hermit asks and he realizes that his frantic searching has detracted him from his real need. He realizes that his rowing has been a noisy distraction from the quiet voice that has been calling him home. It has been a proud preoccupation with self-definition and independent identity. It has been an appeal to Asmodeus, but not to the true King.

The hermit is leading Adam on a journey that is rarely taken by most Christians in the pew. He is inviting him to exit Plato's Cave, to return from Solomon's suburbs, and to enter into a life of total surrender to God's will. The hermit is inviting him to battle the internal dragons of fear that would cause him to begin rowing again. He is inviting him to be consumed by purifying fires. He is inviting him to stagger across desert wilderness and to take up his cross and willingly die.

This is hard for a human will to hear. Even Jesus sweat drops of blood in the garden of Gethsemane, before resolving the issue of "Thy will and not mine be done." Accepting the hermit's invitation will cause the false self to stand up. Then, we will have there, the opportunity to reckon with it—our will behind the wheel of our lives.

The false self, fighting for its life, reruns Satan's rebuttals. "You are getting bad advice. You can have life without death, a resurrection without a cross, and Canaan Land without sore feet." Jesus says you can have Easter morning, but only after Good Friday. He says that abundant life can be yours, but only after you lay down your own life. He says that the promised land is his special gift to us, but only after the wilderness. Jesus, by the example of his life and the work of the cross, makes salvation and a return trip to Eden possible.

But who wants "Good Fridays" or "personal crosses"? Who wants "sore feet" or "wilderness wanderings"? No one. So it's not surprising when Christians desire the milk and honey of their promised land while avoiding hot desert sands. It's not surprising when some are found sitting down and leaning back against the Cairo city limits signpost and singing about how great it is to be in Beulah Land. It's not surprising, just confusing—for those in the world.

For Adam to arrive at a point where he was game for making a decision—radical willingness, for leaving the comfortable signpost, two disciplines were necessary: he had to begin to practice the presence of God as represented by the hermit, and he had to develop a trust in Father God's words—a trust born out of conversation.

Willingness worked. Adam began to make real progress toward home when he took his oars out of the water and held on in his heart to a hope in the kingdom. Like most Christians who have felt the joy of a heartfelt surrender of the will, it was really good for awhile—until a sea monster appeared.

Leap Five: Surviving the Sea Monster

While completing my graduate studies in clinical psychology, I had a part-time job doing psychological testing in a residential treatment center for boys. The boys ranged in age from about seven to seventeen. The majority had been the victims of horrible neglect and abuse. Many of them were like hungry puppies—wide-eyed, constantly in motion, and riveted to anyone who might provide nurture. Others were more hardened and had hair triggers for angry explosions.

One day a small, frail boy came into my office to be tested. He immediately announced, "I ain't afraid of nothing." Being already desensitized to double negatives, I did not think much about his unusual greeting. After some chit-chat to thaw the ice, I began to ask him questions. "How old are you?"

"I'm twelve, and I ain't afraid of nothing."

I was surprised. He looked more like a malnourished nine.

"How long have you been at the center?"

"Just since yesterday, and I ain't afraid of nothing."

"Which cottage are you in?" I asked, finally beginning to see a certain rhythm in his responses.

"I'm in the house with the big guys, but I ain't afraid of them! They ain't so tough!" he proclaimed, this time convincing neither himself nor me.

The questions and, eventually, the testing, continued. During the ensuing two hours, it seemed that he announced his fearlessness at least a hundred times. At least one thing was painfully certain, this poor little fellow, in his new home filled with angry, pimple-faced giants, was one of the most fearful people on the planet. On the outside he was a fearless gun-fighter. On the inside, he was Barney Fife.

The testing to formulate a treatment plan was unnecessary. He was loudly announcing what he needed—to feel safe and secure in the midst of an environment that would cause Rambo to watch his back.

I later learned the ink-and-paper label for what I had observed in the flesh. The frightened little fellow was demonstrating what Freud would call a defense mechanism. Specifically, he was defending his mechanisms with what is called "reaction formation."

A defense mechanism is, of course, a means by which an individual protects himself or herself against unwanted emotions or impulses. A common, but effective defense mechanism is denial. With denial, an individual actively (albeit subconsciously) refuses to admit the reality of an unwanted emotion or impulse.

The "reaction-formation" I had observed in this boy could be described as the finding of relief through the practice and proclamation of the opposite—the antithesis—of the troublesome emotion.

By now you're probably saying, "But, what does this have to do with Adam and the sea monster?" Just like the wide-eyed child I had tested, Adam has been separated from his natural home and is living in the midst of a foreign, fear-producing environment.

Adam and all the rest of us were designed with souls made from the same material as St. Augustine's. Our soul, too, will find no rest until it rests in God.

To thrive, our souls need the nurture afforded by the two highest commandments of Jesus—to give love to and to receive love from fellow humans, and from God. Like the child, Adam is a fish out of water. He is not in his intended environment. He is confused, insecure, fearful, and alone. And like the child, Adam has developed a defense mechanism to muffle these underlying fears and insecurities. But his system of defense is different. He rows. That is, he pursues activities, accomplishments, and achievements as a way to verify himself and to feel more secure. He mistakenly hopes that he can "row" himself "home."

His reaction formation is, "I am important, I am significant. Look at what I have accomplished (look at my rowing)." But, it's like the scared little boy saying, "I ain't afraid." The saying or the doing is the opposite of the real feeling that is going on inside Adam. He becomes convinced by the hermit that he should let go, become willing, and when he does, he drops his defense. Initially, this produces a wonderful feeling of freedom; a feeling that lasts until the shriek of the sea monster rings out.

The sea monster represents an underlying cauldron of emotion—Adam's deepest fears—his feelings of lostness, insecurity, and loneliness produced as a result of being separated from home. As Adam drops his defense, the fears he has been defending himself against now stare him in the face. The "sea monster" is the little boy's fear of being beaten up; and it is Adam's fear that he deserves isolation and eternal separateness.

Adam is in a grave predicament, one that he could remain trapped in for the rest of his life. In the words of the hermit: "Even after experiencing willingness, many travelers spend the remainder of their lives frantically trying to escape from the projected illusions of their own fears."

This sea monster, our most deeply-seated fears, causes many Christians, after brief encounters with willingness, to turn even more feverishly back to their rowing defenses.

Adam's only hope of escaping a ping-pong type of existence (being volleyed back and forth between willing surrender and active self-definition) is to recognize that the sea monster is not real. He must then be willing to accept the refiner's fire which can melt the hardened areas of his heart, the places which give shadowy life to the illusion of a monster, and he must let the light of God's love shine through.

Leap Six: Accepting Personal Crosses

THE FIRE
The dove descending breaks the air
With flame of incandescent terror
Of which the tongues declare
The only hope, or else despair
Lies in the choice of pyre or pyre—
To be redeemed from fire by fire.

Who then devised the torment? Love.
Love is the unfamiliar Name
Behind the hands that wove
The intolerable shirt of flame
Which human power cannot remove.
We only live, only suspire
Consumed by either fire or fire.

T.S. Eliot, "Little Gilding, IV"

Dallas Willard begins his extraordinary book, *The Spirit of the Disciplines*, with the above poem by T.S. Eliot. The poem is an apt beginning for what follows. His central claim is that, "We can become like Christ by doing one thing—by following him in the overall style of life he chose for himself."[7] It is further proposed that following the example of Jesus means participating in the types of activities he practiced, including the practice of the classic Christian disciplines.

Following the path of Jesus, according to Willard, will lead us to a level of transformation which is rarely evidenced in the present-day Christian church. Perhaps there are so few travelers on this road precisely because it inevitably leads to a cross—a cross where the crucifixion of our false self takes place.

M. Scott Peck made a brilliant summation, when articulating earlier observations of Carl Jung, in *The Road Less Traveled.* "Neurosis is always a substitute for legitimate suffering."[8] The term neurosis refers to a disorder of thinking, feeling, or behaving, characterized by a loss of joy in living and overuse of defense mechanisms against anxiety.

In some ways a person experiencing a neurosis can be compared to a person addicted to heroine. Each is likely to be experiencing intense underlying emotional pain. The addict uses a chemical to escape this pain. The neurotic uses subconscious defense mechanisms (often visible to others in the form of subtle patterns of behavior) as a means of escape.

The chemical and the behavioral addict have something in common: each accepts *some* pain so as to avoid a *greater* pain—the legitimate suffering necessary to find freedom. The chemical addict lives with the torture of coming down from repeated drug use to the painful reality of physical suffering (substitute suffering). The emotional addict lives with the torture of coming down from repeated emotional vacations to the painful reality of emotional suffering (substitute suffering). He or she avoids the more excruciating suffering (legitimate suffering) of going "cold turkey" into withdrawal from the drug or emotional addiction. The same pattern of accepting only a little light suffering to avoid the more severe, but ultimately purgative suffering, is present in the neurotic paradigm.

This same pattern is also present for the "spiritually neurotic" Adam. His pain, which each of the first three helpers attempts to lessen, is substitute suffering. The "fire" prescribed by the hermit is provided by love—love that will produce legitimate suffering—cold turkey withdrawal from our substitutes for real love, security, and significance. This same legitimate suffering is referred to in Scripture as "picking up our own personal cross and following Jesus," or as a "refining fire."

Legitimate suffering is prescribed by the desert fathers, who referred to its flames as the "Fire of Love." This legitimate suffering, which our false self views with a deathly fear, is what Dallas Willard calls being "redeemed from fire by fire," and by its flames we may be truly transformed. The hermit is confident in his guidance because he knows that "Love is the unfamiliar name behind the hands that wove the intolerable shirt of flame." A flame that burns the dross in our hearts, leaving only refined gold behind.

Leap Seven: Forgiveness

One evening, while channel-surfing with my family in our den, the face of Don Henley suddenly appeared on the TV screen. Don Henley is the former lead singer for the Eagles. My wife and I, of course, used that teachable moment to help our two children catch up on American life and music in the 70s—and as an excuse to leave the TV parked on that station for a while longer.

The history lesson was soon interrupted by the words and soulful sounds of one of his "newer" songs—"The Heart of the Matter." We all stopped and listened.

My wife said, "I wonder why you don't hear more songs like that in church; I wonder why you have to be watching TV to hear such a heartfelt song about forgiveness?"

None of us knew the answer. We searched our memory banks. We could recall sermons about forgiveness, especially using the passage about leaving your gifts at the altar if there is someone you need to forgive, but we could not recall one song about a Christian coming to terms with his need to "leave the altar" and "forgive."

Now, we didn't conclude that such songs don't exist. We are very aware that we are a musically-challenged family. But we did find it interesting that after sitting for a collective twelve-thousand-plus church services, the best song on forgiveness we had ever heard was being sung in our den by Don Henley.

It seemed a shame. I knew from spending twelve-thousand-plus hours with clients, that forgiveness was at the top of the charts for most-frequently-discussed topics. And from those sessions, I knew that the process of forgiveness—surrendering one's right to be angry, and hurt back—was incredibly difficult to facilitate.

In the rowing analogy, Adam, while on his way to reconciliation, stops in his tracks and pulls an apple from a pocket. He hurls it into the ocean before continuing his journey home. That scene symbolizes the giant leap of forgiveness—an extension of the preceding sixth leap—purgation. I have found forgiveness to be the most often omitted leap as we attempt our journeys back home. We don't want to give up our most tightly held "apple," the desire to hold on to white-hot coals of anger. It's a shame. The leap to reconciliation with God can't be made without it.

You know, someone should write a song.

Leap Eight: Reunion of Reconciliation

When Jesus says, "Make your home in me as I make mine in you," he offers us an intimate place that we can truly call "home." The Christian faith calls us to experience life as "going home" and death as "coming home at last."

Adam, a representative of the rest of us six billion prodigal children, finds his way back home, through the guidance of the Holy Spirit. He completes the circle of the authentic spiritual pilgrimage, so often described as a "journey," in which the self that leaves home—the false self—is not the self that arrives. It is the redeemed true self that makes it home. Adam has made the trek from cave to kingdom, from remote lands to the palace in Jerusalem, from pigpen to his father; and he has fallen once more—back into the arms of a father's love. The drama of the universe is played out on the stage of the human soul.

I saw my friend one more time. While on retreat, we spent a couple of days at the same monastery. It had been more than three years since our last conversation. Around mid-afternoon of the second day, we took a break from all the retreating.

Climbing into a row boat we launched out into a large pond which was in the center of the monastery grounds. Under a clear blue sky, as we drifted in and out of the bright white reflection of the chapel's spire, I listened to my friend recount his journey of the past few years—a journey he had apparently taken under the guidance of the "hermit."

Shortly after our last meeting, he had been given a little paperback book. The book, which contained only fifty to sixty pages, was about the importance of solitude to the life and ministry of Jesus. He had accidentally grabbed it from his study as he was rushing off to the airport one day. Although disappointed when he later discovered that in his haste he had picked up the wrong book, he read it anyway to avoid the in-flight movie.

An hour later, his life had taken a dramatic turn—a turn toward the exit sign at the mouth of Plato's Cave. His life would never be the same. The words of the writer formed a special invitation to begin a life of willingness. It's important to remember that my friend was already a Christian, whom many revered as an anointed prophet. Yet the book, or perhaps it was the Holy Spirit performing the Heimlich maneuver as he read it, convinced him that there was a depth of surrender which he had never allowed himself to explore. There was an invitation to intimacy with God which he had never answered.

In the sixty minutes it took to read the book, hard crystals of cynicism, which had resulted from being constantly reminded of how few Christians act like Christians, began to soften. Maybe, he thought, the promises of an abundant life are really true. Maybe, the main obstacle to finding God's kingdom is not believing that God would actually *desire* intimacy with us.

"It's hard to fathom," my friend said, "that God might actually want me to come out and play with him … that he could want my peace more than my productivity."

Not long after reading the book and making a commitment to willingness, he met a man who had been a spiritual director for a number of years. This fellow was particularly interested in how the orthodox Christian disciplines might be useful to the process of Christian formation. Now, my fortunate companion not only had his oars out of the water, he had an in-the-flesh "hermit" to guide him. And it was a good thing, because his first exposure to real willingness quickly turned nasty.

His first experience was that of a guided retreat. "Do you know what that guy, the director, said to me the first time I was on a directed retreat? Well, I was sitting in his office with a sharp pencil and a legal pad. I said to him, 'Tell me exactly what I need to do to make this retreat stuff work.'

"He looked at me (I'll never forget it) as if to say, 'This is going to be a tough one.' Then he did say, 'Do you remember when you were three or four years old and playing in the back yard?'

"'Yes,' I said. And the memory I had was a pleasant one.

"Did you worry about whether or not there would be a meal on the table or did you just play, having all confidence that at some time you would hear your mother call, 'time to eat?'"

"'I just played,' I said. 'I knew that there would be a meal and that she would call.'

"'Good!' he replied. 'That's exactly how retreats work. You go on out and play. God will call you when it's time to eat.'"

My friend told me that the time period which followed (the next two years) was the most difficult of his life. After he left that office, he found it hard to play. He sat in his room. He walked the grounds. He paced in his room. He paced the grounds. He showed up forty minutes early for lunch and drummed his fingers on a table until it hurt.

He went back to his room and began a routine of alternate pacing and watch-checking. By mid-afternoon he had done everything he knew to do—except play. He got into his car and left without even saying good-bye. He felt he had to escape that place or he would die—never realizing that that was the point.

A month passed before he called to let his director know what had happened. From the perspective of the rowboat in which we sat, he explained to me, "Reading about the ideal of entering into solitude for the purpose of experiencing intimacy with Jesus is one thing. But doing it is another. When I slowed down, horrible, monster-like feelings caught up with me. I didn't want solitude anymore; I didn't want to stop my running. Unfortunately, I already knew too much for the running to be a 'narcotic' for me, anymore."

Deep rooted feelings of fear, inadequacy, and worthlessness (by-products of early compassion deficits he had experienced) continued to grow and bear their rotten fruit. My friend slipped into the flames of hell. He knew his workaholism was a defense against internal pain. Unfortunately, knowing this only served to lessen the narcotic effect of his busy-ness.

But when he slowed down—took his oars out of the water—the fearful feelings of failure caught up and overwhelmed him. He began to cycle back-and-forth between feverish activity and feverish inactivity. The dragon was winning. To make matters worse, his family was beginning to fall apart. His years of absence to go worship at the temple of narcissistic ambition had taken their toll. He was losing his family in a painful and publicly embarrassing fashion.

Then one day, while alone in his empty house, his life crackling and popping in his ears, he cried out to God. "It's over! My life is over! Either kill everything in me which is not in your image or let me die!"

He heard nothing. But a miracle began to happen. He began to die. His false self, which had dominated his whole life, all of his relationships, all his ambitions, became terminally ill. It was a slow, agonizing death. The false self does not live prettily, and it does not die prettily either. He needed help. A few days after his prayer, he initiated contact with his former spiritual director who assisted him in practicing the spiritual disciplines of forgiveness, fasting, intercessory prayer, and quiet, listening prayer. He helped him to distinguish the quiet voice of false self, which made many desperate attempts to regain control.

The seeds of true reconciliation had been planted and would grow. Fruits of restoration began to appear. "All that I had lost was graciously restored," he said as tears streaked his cheeks. "But so much more has been given. I believe in the kingdom like never before. It's a radically different place to live—as different as shadow from substance. And," he said with a playful tone in his voice, "I believe that life can be abundant."

This last statement was interrupted. An elderly monk was waving to us from the shore. It was time to bring the boat back in. It was time for supper. I think we had fish.

4

Shoestrings and Plastic Trophies

Everybody thinks of changing humanity
and nobody thinks of changing himself.

Tolstoy

I looked at the clock. It was right where I had been told a clock in a counseling office should be, midway up the wall, and just behind the client's left ear. The location of the clock would make it easy for me to subtly monitor time during counseling sessions.

I had a long-standing fear that a client would catch me taking a quick glance at my watch just as he was confiding "No one likes to be around me. I really think I am the most boring person on the planet."

"Oh, excuse me," I would say, trying to recover, "but I just can't believe how this session always flies by so much faster than all the rest."

But this perfectly-placed clock would save that embarrassment. My clock even had a sweep second hand—no annoying ticks or clicks to interrupt times of silent reflection. "This is great!" I almost said out loud. There was just one problem: the skinny, black plastic minute hand was about to overtake its slower partner in the vicinity of the five. I was at the halfway point of what should have been my first session with a new client, but I was the only person in the room. It looked like it was to be the third time in a row a client had failed to show.

Certain of another "no show," I allowed myself the luxury of an agitated recline in my crescent-shaped chair. I looked at my shoes. From my horizontal position it was hard to avoid looking at them.

I remembered what a good friend told me in response to my razzing him about an abrupt change in his appearance. His image upgrade coincided with the beginning of his first clinical internship. Overnight, his jeans-and-tennis-shoe look had been replaced by a "GQ"-motif, including shiny silk ties and shoes polished to the point that they had caused me to squint.

"You've got to look successful if you want your clients to believe that you can help them," he explained.

"And to think I have wasted all this time trying to be competent," I responded.

He went on undaunted, "And the most important part of your wardrobe is your shoes."

"Why your shoes?" I had asked, then quickly pursed my lips to keep a snicker from jumping out.

"Because that's what your clients will see most often. They are usually staring at the floor, you know."

My shoes looked pretty bad. Sort of like they had endured Napoleon's early winter, trans-Russia retreat. I make a point of polishing my shoes on an annual basis, whether they need it or not. Somehow this pair, one of my only two, had been overlooked. I glanced back at the clock and then at my dull brown shoes and then at the empty chair where a client should be sitting. I was about to make a connection when I heard a knock at the door.

A quick glance over my shoulder let me know that I was no longer alone in the room. My client had arrived. While I didn't yet realize it, I was about to meet one of the world's most interesting people.

Encounter with a Modern-Day Adam

Bill was halfway across the long, narrow office before I could get my shoes back on the floor and out of his line of vision. He grabbed my hand and shook it vigorously as I was still attempting to dismount. Then he casually plopped down in the other chair with a sense of at-home-ness you would only expect from someone in his own den.

Well, I was the newcomer. He had been making weekly trips to this room for over two years. So I stood there, waiting to make a formal greeting that was now unnecessary.

"Well, there's a lot of ground to cover, so I had better get started," he said. "You see, my last therapist and I were really humming along when we had to stop. We really clicked. You know, he completed his internship and had to move on. Of course you know; he referred me to you. I wish I could have afforded to continue with him, though—no offense. So, anyway, I want to catch you up as fast as I can."

I sucked in a breath to respond, but it was too late. He had already begun. "I was born in a small village in North Dakota. It seems like there was always snow on the ground. At least that's the way I remember it ... "

I immediately liked Bill, even without an apparent reason. As he talked, I was trying to be professionally distant. Uh, I mean neutral, but I couldn't help this totally unfounded, warm first impression.

He had barged into my office and had taken control of it as well as the session. He had shown less social grace than a hungry Chihuahua, but somehow in that first sixty seconds he fostered endearment. It would only grow with time.

Bill was thirty-seven years old. He was of average height, but wore an extra thirty or forty pounds around the middle of his small frame. The extra weight stretched his dark blue polyester pants and caused them to ride up just above the tops of his socks. The bottom two buttons on his shirt were under considerable pressure and failed to conceal his T-shirt, visible as a white, three-dimensional, figure eight. It rested on his belt buckle.

Bill's face seemed friendly and kind, but with a hint of anxiety around his eyes and the corners of his mouth. Round, metal-framed glasses were lodged halfway down a slightly padded nose. His dark, thinning hair was combed back; but a recent re-styling by a stiff September breeze had been ignored. His appearance brought to mind a manic teddy bear. I didn't think he would be offended by my shoes.

"I don't have that many memories before age three. I'm sure that's normal, wouldn't you say. I'm sure it is," he said, not waiting for my response. "My father was a kind man, but he was a real disciplinarian.... "

Bill was an eager historian of his life. This was his third year as a client at the clinic. Reams of documentation suggested that he was also a consistent one. He had been born in a remote corner of North Dakota, near the Canadian border. He was the oldest of five children begat by hard working, "fundamentalist" (his word) parents.

From his descriptions, it sounded as if they lived in such an outlying area that his father would have to drive toward town if he wanted to hunt. But I doubt he would have allowed himself the pleasure. Bill described his section of North Dakota as a cold, harsh, wind-swept place. "If you had any money at all, you escaped the winters." Bill didn't know anyone who escaped.

When he turned his attention to describing the environment inside his home, he painted the picture of an orderly and controlled atmosphere that, at an emotional level, mirrored the rest of the land's cold and barren surroundings.

He grew up in fear. He breathed it in with every breath like thick smog. "I was constantly afraid that Jesus was coming back and that I would be left behind. I can't tell you the number of times I came home to an empty house and panicked thinking that the rapture had occurred and I had been left behind. My mother would usually be the one to find me running around outside wringing my hands and dropping tears on my shirt. She would grab me, and holding me at arm's length she would say, 'Everything is fine, Billy, we're here … this time. Maybe the Lord's just trying to tell you to make sure you don't have any sin in your life.' Even while being comforted I felt afraid."

Bill's father was a hardworking man, the strong, silent no-nonsense type. Bill always assumed that he was loved by his father, which was probably very true, but there was little supporting evidence. His father was consumed with other, apparently more important, matters.

In affairs of the home, his mother's advances were equal to his father's retreats and this produced a strikingly matriarchal family. She ruled the roost, and one of her most strictly enforced rules was that the family had to be in church every time the doors were opened. They were.

She was a very orderly, perfectionist woman who kept the small, modestly furnished home in such a fashion that it could pass anyone's "white glove test." She set out to make sure that the souls of her children could also pass such an inspection. It never occurred to her that love could be used as a miracle whitener. She saw to it that her children would live lives that would bring a nod of approval from even the strictest of the "Pharisees."

At age thirty-seven, Bill took obvious pride in saying, "No alcohol has ever touched these lips and no profane word has ever passed them." Because Bill appeared so anxious, I must admit that, even as a fully fundamental fundamentalist myself, I had to suppress the perverse suggestion, "Well, Bill, why don't you just down a quick six-pack, challenge a couple of sailors to a cursing match, and call me in the morning? I think you'll feel a lot better." But, clearer thinking, and remembering that my supervisor would be reviewing audiotapes from the session prevented that particular intervention.

Bill's father was a non-enthusiastic participant in the "Christian education" of his children. "He complied," Bill said, "but I must admit I often wondered if his heart was really in it."

A thick film of guilt clung to the fear-filled air of Bill's childhood home. He included the following story in his "historical overview," without even pausing for a breath, or the reflection that it deserved.

"This is an odd memory. It is one of my first memories. I must have been about three. I remember running while carrying my mother's favorite blue vase. I had found a flower for her outside. I went in and got the vase, and I was running to the well to put some water in it." His face became still and somber but he immediately continued. "Then I fell. The vase slipped from my hand and shattered into pieces. Without even thinking, I reached down and grabbed one of my shoestrings and broke it and I started crying, almost hysterically, 'It's not my fault! It's not my fault!'"

"You broke the string ... so you wouldn't be blamed?" His eyes filled with mist, he nodded as he formed the words of the next line of his story. "My next memory was of when I was four." He went on without me. I wasn't following what he was saying because I wanted to stop and cry. Neither Bill nor I knew that he had just described one of the most important paradigms of his life (self-punishment administered to allay his guilt); one of several deeply-rooted patterns of behavior which were the subtle but primary reasons he was sitting in my office. I mentally caught up with Bill a few memories downstream.

"I was painfully shy in school." Apparently he had very few close friends. Some students he actively avoided because he was afraid their "worldliness" might smudge his "holiness" if they got too close. Others he passively avoided because he was so certain of their rejection. "I always related more easily with adults. I knew how to make them like me."

Indeed he did. He threw himself into the pursuit of academic accomplishments usually earning straight As, and every certificate, merit badge, and plastic trophy that the small country school could afford to hand out. "With all the awards I won in school, it was easy for Mother to win the bragging competitions at our family reunions," he said, beaming like a five year old making a maiden voyage on a bike. Bill began to believe at a very early age that his value as a person was one and the same with his productivity. He was given very little evidence to dispute this belief.

In my second session with Bill he told me about the death of his father. "I was twelve when my father died. He had been diagnosed as having leukemia just a few months earlier. We knew for more than a year that something was wrong. He would stay in bed a few extra minutes each morning. That wasn't like him at all; and he would let me do things—you know, things that required strength—that he used to do himself. I remember that, for a while, I thought he was letting me show off some of the muscles I was developing. But it wasn't that. He was slowly dying. I always thought he was too strong to die, but he wasn't that strong after all. I really loved him. I think he loved me too."

To me, the word "think" came out of Bill's mouth in bold-faced type.

Not long after the death of his father, Bill's mother remarried a strict, fundamentalist minister whose wife had recently left him. It remains a mystery how she found someone in such a remote area who mirrored her cold, militaristic view of child raising. Bill, still bleeding from gaping wounds caused by the shearing away of his father, redoubled his efforts to be a perfect son and a perfect Christian. On the surface, he was remarkably successful.

Unfortunately for Bill, the quality of human relationships is more dependent upon subterranean formations and activities than on a polished upper-crust. This twelve-year-old, polished-at-the-surface Pharisee had many pockets of rotting debris in numerous, not so remote, caverns of his psyche. Over time the foul odor from these pockets of decay (and the various methods he used to mask the stench) would bubble up and become apparent at the surface. This unfortunate fact would cost him three marriages and numerous jobs, and caused him almost unfathomable pain. It was the reason he was now in my office. It was the reason he hardly knew that I was also present.

A Case for Spiritual Malpractice:
Apply the Wisdom of the First Three Helpers

I met with Bill on a weekly basis as time flew by. He never once caught me glancing in the direction of his left ear to see the clock. Surely he must have thought that my circadian rhythms pulsated with the precision of a Greenwich timepiece, because during each session at precisely 5:49 P.M., I would say something like, "This sounds like an important issue. Perhaps you will want to continue from this point next week."

Through trial and embarrassment I have learned that one must be careful to make sure an important issue has in fact been raised before placing that particular "colon" at the end of a session. If, for instance, a client observes at 5:49, "I believe that is the biggest ball of carpet lint I have ever seen. It looks like a Texas tumbleweed," then, some other session-ending phrase must be substituted.

Anyway, back to our story. Just beyond Bill's other ear was the third most important piece of equipment in a counseling office. (I have already discussed the clock and mentioned the chairs.) It is the mental health disease identification Bible known as the *Diagnostic and Statistical Manual of Mental Disorder*. It was encased by dull green covers and held erect by two imitation-brass, horse-head bookends. Sitting where I could readily see it, the book frequently caught my attention during sessions with Bill and reminded me of my resolve to memorize its contents during my two years of internship training.

The *DSM* represented the mental health branch of a gigantic disease classification tree which is published in multiple volumes as the *International Classification of Disease* (ICD), by the World Health Organization (WHO).

The ICD offers a numeric classification system using the numbers 000.001 to 999.999, as labels for each and every known medical malady. It was helpful to me to think of it as the Dewey Decimal System for cataloging diseases. Everything from ingrown toenails (703.0) to myocardial infarctions (410.9) and from parietal lobe aneurysm (437.3) to carpet-lint hair balls in the esophagus (933.0)—I'm not kidding here— are listed and numerically labeled in the ICD.

The international use of the disease classification system assures that whether you are coughing and wheezing in Athens, Georgia or Athens, Greece, if your condition is diagnosed as 933.0, you have a tickle in your esophagus—probably caused by an unexpected inhale while closely inspecting a carpet-lint hair ball. 301.13 was Bill's number. I found it on page 218 of that particular edition of the manual, along with a 500-word essay describing his "disorder."

It took several sessions with Bill, careful review of a two-year collection of session notes, consultation with a supervisor, and basic deductive reasoning with my copy of the *DSM* to arrive at this number, which best described Bill's condition. While my speed would increase in the coming years, there would be no improving on the accuracy. It was a bull's eye.

Bill was clearly suffering from a mental health condition known as "cyclothymia." That is, for years he had cycled back and forth and up and down, between depression and depression's polar opposite, mania. Like a roller coaster in ultra slow motion he would descend into the shadow of a long dark tunnel known as major depression (296.23), but he never quite entered the tunnel. Then he would slowly ascend to a level of normality and he would rise above the level of normality to the lofty heights of mania, but never high enough for the diagnosis of manic episode (296.40) to perfectly fit. Bill rode an emotional roller coaster through life. He was never diagnostically depressed, never diagnostically manic, and never diagnostically normal. His lows were too low, his highs too high, and his moderates were short-lived.

When Bill made his initial visit to the clinic, two years prior to the time I first saw him, he was at the very bottom of the depressed cycle. At that time, his dress was very casual, almost sloppy. He spoke softly, never interrupted the therapist, and often allowed tears to flow out of his despair. He complained of mild sleeping difficulties ("I just want to stay in bed all morning.") and attempted to mute an internal cry of remorse for some unspecified loss, with muffling mounds of rich desserts (he ate a lot when he was depressed).

The Bill who strutted across my office that early evening in September had recently been to the heights of hypomania and was poised, gripping the sides of his cart, at the top of his highest, white-wooden-skeleton hill, about to begin another downward descent into despair. His speech was still rushed and somewhat pressured. Listening to Bill brought to mind the idea of trying to sip water from a fire hydrant. The listener often felt pushed back by a spray of words and ideas which traveled too fast for human interaction.

Even with another downward descent in clear view, Bill was still high. He was staying up later than David Letterman and arising before Willard Scott. Mind and body still marched double time, but sundown was in sight. The Bill of those September sessions was like shooting fireworks, offering one last spectacular display of sounds and lights before giving in to the inevitable grasp of gravity. Bill's eyes sparkled and popped, even as depression once again reached up to pull down the corners of his mouth. His high had been *too* high. His low would soon be *too* low.

301.81. That was Bill's other number. He had prominent traits of what is known in the *DSM* series as a Narcissistic Personality Disorder. This is a condition more of character and constitution than biochemistry. It derives its name from the myth of Narcissus—a story which has endured as a warning against self-absorption.

Like Narcissus, Bill's vision was riveted to his own reflection. His thoughts were dominated by grandiose fantasies of unlimited success and recognition. He showed a pronounced lack of empathy for the feelings and needs of others. At times I was left with the impression that Bill thought he was the center of the universe. At others times, I believe, he thought he *was* the universe.

I must confess that listening to Bill talk often brought to mind a character who used to be part of the Saturday Night Live ensemble, Al Frankin. Al Frankin was a modern day Narcissus who was unabashedly egocentric. His skit usually followed a parody of the week's news, and he always began his monologue with the same formula. For example, following a "news" segment on the four hundred hostages held in Iran, Al would say something like, "I guess you are all wondering how the taking of American hostages by Iran affects me, Al Frankin. Well, I'll tell you.… "

Bill was a caring and compassionate person, but he was like a man wearing blinders in a mirror-filled room. Most of the time he saw only himself. References to others in his life was like Al Frankin's references to the hostages and went something like, "I guess you're wondering how my wife's new job affects me, Bill." Bill rode an emotional roller coaster through a house of mirrors. It was no wonder that almost all the relationships in his life had failed.

Advice from the First Two Helpers

In the opening allegory in chapter one, the first two characters who try to help Adam represent two dominant schools of psychological intervention—behavioral and cognitive psychotherapy. They offer suggestions to Adam who is lost at sea and in much physical, mental, and spiritual pain.

The method of help I extended to Bill was copied from the logs of these two helpers—I went by the book. I helped Bill to "row" more efficiently—to make positive behavioral changes—and I armed him to do battle with tortuous thoughts. As you will see, I did very little to help. This is the way it went.

By the Book

Step 1: Determine if the client is currently a danger to himself or others. Is there evidence to suggest he is at high risk for self harm (suicide)? Is he a danger to others (homicidal)? Or is he gravely disabled concerning self-care? Careful, direct questioning during the initial session, a review of his chart, and a discussion with his most recent therapist, provided sufficient information to determine he did not need to be hospitalized.

Step 2: Determine a diagnosis using the *DSM*. As I already said, Bill met the diagnostic criteria for cyclothymia and showed prominent traits of a Narcissistic Personality Disorder. There was evidence that he was about to enter into the depressed phase of his cyclical mood disturbance.

Step 3: If warranted by diagnosis, refer the patient for medical evaluation concerning the appropriateness of psychiatric medication. We did that and it was determined that lithium (a frequently prescribed medication for individuals suffering from an extremely elevated mood—mania) was not indicated. In fact, no psychiatric medication was indicated. Later, when Bill's symptoms of depression became more pronounced, an antidepressant was prescribed. Bill's depressive symptoms (hyposomnia, depressed mood, increased appetite, loss of energy) showed a modestly positive response to medication.

Let me be clear about where I stand on medication for psychological symptoms. In my mind, the taking of such medications do not preclude the need for "psychological" intervention. After all, a person who develops pneumonia from spending the winter in Alaska in a house with no furnace and gaping holes in the floor and walls may need both hospitalization and medication ... and he needs to move. Bill's physician gave him the appropriate medication. I set out to help him "move."

Step 4: Consult the recent literature in psychology to determine what has proven to be the most effective intervention for individuals who suffer from similar conditions. What has worked for others who have been assigned the numbers 296.23 and 301.81?

Step 5: Implement those interventions which have proven to be effective. With Bill, this step proved difficult to accomplish. The treatment of cyclothymia is not well defined in the psychiatric-psychological literature. If the hypomanic cycle is currently predominating, lithium may be prescribed. If depression is the chief mood disturbance an anti-depressant might be prescribed. The third recommended treatment for cyclothymia is to help the client evaluate his social and family situations to determine if there are tempestuous life events. If there are, he may find relief from these situations through behavioral or cognitive change strategies. This third option brings us, then, to the advice of the first two helpers.

As part of his evaluation process, I instructed Bill to monitor his moods several times each day. I asked him to assign a numeric rating (something like zero being "yucky" and ten being "ecstatic"). For each entry on his mood rating form he was to answer certain journalistic "who," "what," "where," and "when" questions. This type of exercise not only provided documentation pertaining to the rise and fall of his emotions, but it also furnished rich details concerning the people, events, thoughts, and behaviors that are repeatedly found in close proximity to those moods.

Our use of a mood-monitoring strategy led to a variety of other interventions. When it was clearly evident that poor communication with his wife, which almost always involved a lack of empathy with her feelings and desires, was a frequent precursor to verbal battles, loss of intimacy, and subsequent feelings of depression; marital communication training became a focus for our counseling. I could almost hear the voice of the "first helper" in my ear, "Yes, Bill, change the way that you row and your pain will be cut in half." He did, and it was.

Bill's mood-monitoring records also revealed numerous episodes of sadness which followed closely on the heels of interchanges with his employer. It appeared that Bill's desperate desire to please, led him frequently to promise the moon. But he was often unable to keep his promises and Bill would then become quite angry at himself for making them. He would also become angry with his boss for expecting delivery on the promises. He would make faces, frequently exaggerating the angle of his boss' frown or he would put words in his boss' mouth. His creative unspoken criticisms led to further feelings of alienation and depression.

We observed another flaw in Bill's rowing behavior and suggested assertion training as a corrective. That, too, helped. Then we realized that Bill engaged in very few pleasant behaviors. Suggesting to a depressed individual that he needs to do more fun things is tantamount to telling a drowning person that he needs dry land. It's true, but not very helpful. However, "pleasant event scheduling" is a frequently prescribed behavioral change for depressed individuals.

In using pleasant events scheduling, the patient identifies at least twenty fun things he likes to do, or used to like to do in the past. Then, the counselor encourages the patient to make himself engage in several of those behaviors each day. This prescription was tailor-made for Bill. He gave it a try and it proved successful in causing a modest upturn in the slope of his mood-monitoring graph.

Finally, Bill was introduced to the idea of cognitive restructuring. As we explained in chapter two, this is a process of identifying the key maladaptive thoughts that are frequent precursors to painful emotions. This procedure of cognitive reorientation was applied to a cluster of "automatic thoughts" associated with Bill's feelings of depression as well as to certain narcissistic attitudes which hindered intra- and interpersonal relationships. The "captain's" suggestions were also somewhat helpful. By mid-winter, Bill had learned to row his boat with increased efficiency and decreased pain. His distress, caused by tormenting self-talk, was also on the decline. But after all of that, he was still lost at sea. He was still a long way from home. He was still destined to traverse the same course. I was a young therapist in desperate need of a supplemental book. I needed answers.

May I Have Another Book, Please?

"So, you're down to the last week with Bill," Hal said. "I can't believe how this year has flown by. It seems like just yesterday, well, last week anyway, that you were starting sessions with him. My, my, it does fly by. Well, you must feel pretty good about the work you two have done."

Hal was my supervisor. He was a tall, thin, middle-aged man of Germanic descent. He had the wiry body of a marathon runner and precise features. He looked a lot like the images of "Jack Sprat" that I, as a child listening to nursery rhymes, had filed away, so much so that I often wondered about his eating habits. But, regardless of who licked the platter clean, Hal had been an excellent supervisor. He was compassionate, affirming, and very knowledgeable.

He sat patiently, waiting for my response. I looked at him for a long moment. Sunlight reflected from the center of his polished dome, as his eyes searched my face for a response.

"I feel OK about the progress Bill has made," I finally said.

Hal's trained ear heard the hesitancy in my voice. "Just OK. Just OK? This man was seriously messed up nine months ago," Hal said, cutting to the heart of the *DSM*. "He's a different person than he was when you first saw him. Lower your expectations, son. You did good! You could probably get a journal article out of this one."

I couldn't deny that it had gone by the book. I knew that now Bill would show up significantly more stable on an emotional Richter scale. But I also had a nagging suspicion that the psychological intervention I had initiated, had not penetrated beneath the surface of his life any farther than the legalistic interventions his mother had prescribed when he was a child. I was also suspicious that a good portion of his changed behavior was motivated by a desire to be a "perfect" client. I think he would have stood on his head if I had told him that is what good clients did to get better—especially if I had said that he did it better than anyone else.

I thanked Hal for his affirmation and for the free advice about lowering expectations, but I was a hopeless idealist. I stood a better chance of winning a Russian lottery than of lowering my expectations. Final sessions with Hal and Bill would come quickly, but I would never really terminate with either of them.

More than half an hour after the clock indicated that our last counseling session was over, I found myself on the receiving end of a bear hug from Bill. "Thanks," he said with a quivering voice. "I can't tell you what you have done for me." He wiped away tear streaks from both cheeks with the cuffs of his sleeves, turned, and walked to the door. Giving a final wave and a wet glance, he disappeared. I never saw him again.

I sat at my desk, jotted down a quick session note, and put off writing the termination summary for another day. I left the clinic and walked slowly through the moon-like glow of the street lights. Halfway home I stopped at my favorite place to think. It's a homey, grease-based, fast food restaurant that features a three-pound burrito. I passed on the lifetime supply of saturated fat, and ordered an oversized cup of coffee. (It was impossible to leave that place with the same life-expectancy with which you entered.)

I sat, and drank coffee, and thought. My whole approach to counseling was about to be forever altered, and in less time than it took to reach the generous supply of coffee grounds resting at the bottom of my cup.

Whispers from a Hermit

For some reason my mind drifted back to thick, hot August days in rural Georgia and walking on sun-baked, tar and gravel roads. (Maybe it was the coffee that made me remember.) I thought about the "tar-bubbles" that would ooze up from gummy deposits below like bubbles blown from licorice gum. I remembered that on days when it was too hot for baseball and we'd left the beavers to dam the creek, my friends and I would occasionally pass time by popping those tar-bubbles with a stick. Well, most of us used sticks. Once Bobby Johnson used his finger and got introduced to that bar of sand known as Lava soap. My memory of tar oozing up explained my dissatisfaction. I felt that my work with Bill had been the equivalent of observing and popping those black bubbles.

Bill hadn't shown such deep and emotional gratitude because I had given him significant help. He had simply appreciated a friend with whom he had shared time—and a stick. I had left Bill with unfinished business. Huge tar deposits were still prominent. He had no idea where they were coming from. And, the next heat wave in his life would cause more bubbles to appear. In the next moment I became convinced that I knew the source of the bubbles.

Bernie Segal, in his book *Love, Laughter, and Medicine*, stated that, "All disease is ultimately related to a lack of love."[1] He further asserts that the source of all healing is love. While I cannot attest to the orthodoxy of Dr. Segal's faith, reading his words caused a light bulb to suddenly glow inside my head. Love is the lubricating oil of inter- and intrapersonal relationships.

Perhaps each diagnosis in the *DSM*, at one level, simply represents ways and patterns by which individuals respond to compassion deficits—love omitted, or rejection committed. Perhaps the *DSM* I was committing to memory was the equivalent of a mechanic's manual describing the different noises a car makes when it has been run without enough oil.

With Bill I had been popping these pockets-of-nothing which arose from a deep and significant source—injuries caused by the absence of love. Or perhaps it would be better to say that he had come in with a noisy engine and I helped him—gave him more octane and prescribed custom-fit earmuffs.

Central to Bill's cyclothymia was the concept of lost love and lost acceptance. His lows were always triggered by rejection (present reminders of lost love) and his highs were always inflated with expanding anticipation of love regained. Bill showed striking traits of narcissism, but so does a man with a recently severed limb. Each may be self-absorbed and show a diminished capacity to take the needs of others into account.

Like a person who has experienced catastrophic physical trauma, Bill was unable to free himself from the grip of his own injury. The needs of others seemed trivial. Unlike a person with a severed limb, however, Bill's deep injury—his loss of love— had not healed with time, not even with the passing of three decades. Perhaps this was because he had been treating his injury with emotional narcotics and layers of gauze.

I then thought of the time I had asked Bill to bring in all his "narcotics." He complied and brought in a large, cardboard box, filled to its tattered brim with the "drugs" he used to mask his pain.

During our first ten sessions, Bill had dominated the airwaves with tales (tall tales, I had suspected) of his past accomplishments, honors, and awards. He had earned a Ph.D., written a "critically-acclaimed" book, seen his name in print in newspapers all over the world, owned priceless collections, and received the equivalent of "standing ovations" for his skills in the bedroom. Quite frankly I had not believed him. I had endured long hours of his pontificating monologues while patiently nodding, grunting, and stifling yawns.

I was sure that his boasts were nothing more than thinly veiled delusions of grandeur. After I had located that section in the *DSM*, I began to wonder if we would ever move on to more relevant material. Finally, in what I thought was a stroke of therapeutic genius, I confronted Bill and told him I thought he was using these stories to avoid the real process of therapy.

While never letting on that I doubted the veracity of his accomplishments, I encouraged him to bring in all the "trophies" he had been describing to a designated session in which we would celebrate these accomplishments. After that such talk would be out of bounds for our time together.

To my absolute surprise he agreed. The following week he brought in a cardboard trophy case (an old banker's box) which contained all the evidence to back up all of his claims (except for the ones about standing ovations, but by that point I was red-faced and ready to concede that one as well). They were all true!

Bill spent that hour in apparent rhapsody. With careful hands that caressed each object as if it were a thin-shelled egg, he unpacked the box. He cried. He laughed. He crowed. Beams of pride shone from his face as he described each item with the thoughtfulness and shameless immodesty of a grand-mother talking about her grandchildren.

While I was struck too dumb with amazement to draw the connection, Bill was doing much more than walking down memory lane. In his hands he held the precious, tangible, "narcotics" (vials of pain-relieving elixir) that he used to mask the anguish caused by a cancer that ate away at his very being. The absence of love and the constant focus on his "sin and unworthiness" had produced a deadly carcinogen in Bill's psyche. It produced a cancer that ate away at the very fabric of his being.

Bill had begun to treat himself at a very young age. He had learned to wrap his pain with the gauze of denial. He had also discovered that he could treat the pain with his precious accomplishments, honors, and awards. In Bill's mind, he *was* what he produced. He had sold his birthright for porridge dished out by the raters and grade givers of the world. While I had been scraping off skin cancers (popping tar bubbles) and muffling the noise, a deadly cancer had continued its destruction. Neither of us had seen it. Neither of us knew what to do about it.

As M. Scott Peck expresses in *People of the Lie*, "Whenever there is a major deficit in parental love, the child will, in all likelihood, respond to that deficit by assuming itself to be the cause of the deficit, thereby developing an unrealistically negative image."[2]

Clearly, I thought as I was getting to the bottom of my cup, Bill had experienced major compassion deficits. He had assumed blame and an unrealistic negative image of himself. He fought his loss with a narcissistic self-absorption and a box full of "drugs." But what had happened to his true-self—the *imago dei*—which surely had residence somewhere beneath his tightly stretched skin?

"Oh my!" I said just before the coarse coffee grounds began to slide down my throat, "Bill told me."

The unpleasant taste in my mouth duplicated that of my memory, as I recalled an interchange I had with Bill a few months earlier. Not too many weeks after the "trophy-box" session, Bill began to backslide. That is, he again began to slip into monologues about his honors and accomplishments. At one point after my fourth or fifth reminder about our agreement to avoid such testimonials, Bill became uncharacteristically testy, and blurted out, "All right! You want to know more about my insides? Well, I'll tell you. I'll take you inside my 'holy-of-holies'!" We had the following dialogue.

Me: (in response) "You'll take me inside your 'holy-of-holies'?"

Bill: "Yeah, I'm not afraid to do that."

Me: "I'm really not sure I'm following you."

Bill: "I'm talking about the innermost part of who I am. Deep inside I am a little boy who sits in a room behind a veil. Who sits next to a big gold box."

Me: "You are that little boy?"

Bill: "Yes, I am that boy, and I am the one that keeps him locked deep within."

Me: "Does he want to come out?"

Bill: "Of course, he wants to come out."

Me: "But you won't let him come out?"

Bill: "He stays in because he is so afraid of being rejected. He cannot be rejected again or he will die. He sits alone by the golden box."

Me: "What do you suppose is inside the box?"

Bill: "I don't know."

Me: "Why don't you let him look in to see."

Bill: (After a long delay and with tears in his eyes.) "There is a robe and a crown in the box—and a mirror."

Me: "You're crying, Bill. What are you feeling?"

Bill: "That little boy is a prince. He is sitting imprisoned in that small place, and he's a prince."

Me: "So what would happen if he put on the robe and crown and left the room?"

Bill: "He can't!"

Me: "Why not?"

Bill: "There is a guard outside."

Me: "A guard, how do you know?"

Bill: "I see his shadow through the veil."

Me: "Are you afraid?"

Bill: "Yes!"

I let both Bill and me off the hook and allowed the subject to be changed. Bill had made his point. He wasn't afraid to occasionally look within, but it was obviously unpleasant, and he preferred to avoid it.

From the first interchange, I had felt uncomfortable. At that point in my therapeutic career, if a patient and I were dealing with material that did not directly relate to diagnosis, empathetic understanding, or behavioral and cognitive change strategies, I felt that I was inviting a malpractice suit. As Bill and I talked, words like, "interesting," "Freudian," "let's back out of this," flashed through my mind.

I think I filed away a mental note about the "golden box" probably representing his "trophy box," and that the "shadow" was likely a mental picture of his fear of rejection.

I even entertained the idea that he had concocted the whole thing to prove his virility as a good client. But I never entertained the thought that entered my mind that night as I sat in the restaurant.

The isolated boy who sat next to the box that contained the robe and the crown was Bill's "true self." The shadowy guard who kept him prisoner was his "false self," a self that stayed alive only so long as it could keep the true self from the "throne."

I swallowed hard, tossed my cup into a grimy trash can, and walked back out into the night. It would be a long time before books, friends, clients, and personal experience would bring me into contact with the "hermit" and his wisdom concerning willingness, sea monsters, and the fiery flames which were often involved in the emancipation of the true self.

However, even as I walked toward home that night, I was already convinced of one thing. Therapy was a much more dynamic and spiritual process than I had ever imagined. If I were going to be a therapist, I would have to put down my stick, give up the safety of distance, and jump into the tar pit.

I just hoped there would be enough Lava soap to get me clean again.

5

The Last Major Detour

The best victory is to conquer self.

Proverb

The squealing brakes of a chicken truck awoke me from a pleasant daydream. I glanced out my office window and saw thick diesel smoke being coughed out from a blackened smokestack. The smokestack was banging against a rusty cab, making more noise than a hyperactive blacksmith. The driver, coughing out smoke of his own, tugged at the bill of a grimy baseball cap, while waiting for the light to change colors again.

Wooden cages were stacked seven layers deep on the bed of the truck. Each over-packed cage held bewildered chickens that scanned an unfamiliar landscape, their heads bobbing and jerking as if loaded on springs. It was obviously their first trip into town—and their last. They would be frozen and wrapped in plastic. It was enough to make any sensitive person become a vegetarian.

The sight of a chicken truck caused me to recall a conversation with a friend from Long Island. We were both living in Los Angeles at the time.

"You mean youwah home town is so small that it does not even have a movie theatah?" he asked, unaware that he had asked the question without the benefit of the letter "r."

"Yep," I said.

"What did you guys do on Saturday nights afta you went out fowah pizza?" he said, looking at me as if I had suddenly put on a coonskin cap.

"We didn't have a restaurant that served pizza, so it was never a problem."

"Well," he went on, "How faw did you have to drive to get to a city that had a movie theatah?"

"Well, Athens was about thirty miles away," I answered.

"Thirty miles?" he said, emphasizing the word miles. "No, tell me in minutes so I will know how faw it really is."

"OK, then, about forty minutes. Unless, of course, you get behind a chicken truck; then it can take half a day."

"A chicken truck?"

"Never mind," I said. "Let's talk about the Knicks."

The light changed and the chicken truck jerked itself into motion, perhaps making the half-day trip to Athens. I looked at the clock—the polished, brass one in my pseudo Williamsburg-styled office. I had come a long way since the cracked-vinyl and poster-print days of an intern.

It would be almost an hour before my next client was scheduled to arrive. I stared at the written records that had preceded her to my office. I couldn't believe that I had agreed to see someone on a Friday.

One of the ways I had reconciled starting a private practice was to promise myself, my wife and child, and anyone else in earshot, that I would not work on Fridays. Never!

"Every weekend will be three days long," I had repeatedly reassured them. But student loans, small business loans, and the lack of a retirement plan had a way of shrinking the weekend back down to its standard size. I had no idea that the arrival of a new baby would soon make it disappear completely.

I had been in private practice for about six months. It was my distinction to be the first clinical psychologist in Royston,

Georgia. Well, at least the first to stay longer than it takes to eat a plate full of fried chicken at one of the local restaurants, or to bolt in and out of a courtroom as an expert witness. In fact, at that time, I was the only psychologist in a five-county area. It was no wonder that business had been booming.

Feeling no strong desire to review the case records, I put on a new reel of daydreams. My mind drifted back to internship days in California. It had been almost two years since I had seen Bill's round face disappear for the last time into a dimly-lit hallway (chapter four). But its image was still bright and flickering in my memory. After all, how could I forget the face of the man who had thrown my life into such a tailspin?

There had been a definite message on his face that evening. It was as conspicuous as a flashing neon beer sign on a Southern Baptist church. It read, as it circled his head, "THANK YOU ... BUT I THOUGHT MENTAL HEALTH WOULD FEEL A WHOLE LOT BETTER THAN THIS." I don't think Bill knew any better than to confuse mental health with spiritual health. I had helped him travel up the "normal curve" from abnormal pain to normality. But he wanted to slide down the other side—to abnormal levels of love, peace, and joy.

My failure to further help Bill had stuck in my heart like a splinter. Shortly after he walked away from my office, I walked away from psychology—for more than a year—and searched for someone to pull the splinter out. The search had failed, but the pain from that wound remained with me. It was no wonder that my inability to escort Bill back to "Eden" had caused me so much misery. After all, by that point in my life, I had already made a sizable investment so that I could help people like him find their way back home.

At the tender age of twenty-three I had somehow convinced my wife that we should cram all of our worldly belongings into the cold, metal mouth of a U-Haul truck and have ourselves an adventure in moving—2,352 miles to the west. I purposefully kept it to myself that as a child I had experienced considerable difficulty being away from home for a full week of summer camp.

I was determined to make that pilgrimage, which would allow me to spend the remainder of my twenties studying clinical psychology and theology, at the graduate level, so that I would be able to spend the remainder of my life helping people find their lost Edens. I was looking for mine, too. I'm not sure what my wife was supposed to get out of the deal, but she offered gracious support to the quest.

After five grueling days on the road and one mangled car bumper (Now I know that it is very important to leave the key in the ignition of a towed car), the next phase of the adventure began. We coughed and wheezed our way through the unpacking of that truck as our lungs became lined with grime from the smog-infested air of Southern California.

We both cried ourselves to sleep that night wondering if the six years we had planned to spend there would be enough time for our oxygen-starved bodies to unpack the boxes which were piled all around us like a messy child's blocks.

The next day, while standing in a checkout line at a nearby grocery store—one that didn't have the food shelved in logical places, like the stores in Georgia, I said to Jeanie, my wife, "You know, we'll have to stand in this line 311 more times before we can go back home to Georgia." We both started crying again, and I promised to stop doing math in public.

But as quickly as things had turned sad, they turned joyful again. We both settled into a glorious six-year period of adventure—a kaleidoscope of new friends, thoughts, ideas, and dreams. The school I had chosen to attend lived up to all its advance billing, and with time we were able to wean our taste buds from Spam to tofu and unpack most of the boxes.

During my six years as a student of Christian psychotherapy I earned a Ph.D. in clinical psychology and an M. Div. in theology. I logged close to four hundred graduate hours and invested more than a quarter of a million dollars (counting six years of lost wages) in the quest to be a Christian psychotherapist.

I had studied Rogerian techniques from a gifted teacher so "warm and nondirective" he made Carl Rogers look like an impatient sadist. I had received instruction in behavioral techniques from someone who thought B. F. Skinner was far too feeling-oriented. I learned how to analyze transactions, put alter-egos into "empty chairs," and engage clients in dialogue with their "shadows."

I studied the writings of the heroes of psychotherapy from Freud to Ellis, and from Lazarus to May. Somehow (through a paper-shuffling snafu no doubt), I had been selected for a very competitive internship program, and during that experience I had often spent eight hours per week in one-on-one supervision with many of the contributors to the *DSM*. But even after receiving the very best of training from a truly remarkable school, I still couldn't help Bill find his way back to "Eden."

Just weeks before passing the National Board Exam for Psychologists, I *still* couldn't provide Bill with the direction he needed. I wasn't even sure I knew how to get to Eden. I did know that I had never been there.

Well, I reasoned, if psychology could not provide the answer, there was only one thing to do. We must go and live with people who knew the way back to Eden. So, we set out to do just that. We sold, or gave away, most of our worldly possessions, loaded the remainder on an east-bound U-Haul truck (of much smaller dimensions than the original) and headed back home to Georgia.

From there we went to France where we spent time living in community with the Brothers of the Community of Taizé (the world's only collection of reformed-protestant monks). Fortunately, my wife and I had planned a week-long "trial-run" before moving into the monastic community with our high expectations and our two-year-old daughter.

During that fact-finding week our hearts were warmed by the brothers and the retreatants at that miraculous community. Our spirits soared. However, our derrieres contracted frostbite. As our frozen parts thawed, our thinking improved. It slowly dawned on us that the physical conditions were too Spartan for our two-year-old daughter. Our thirty-year-old bodies sang the Hallelujah Chorus in tribute to reason.

But, before we could tell them, they told us. The rough translation from French to English was. "A married couple living with monks could be as distracting as croissants at a weight-watchers meeting," or something to that effect. We understood and confessed that our intuition had probably outrun our reason. We packed our frozen toothpaste and headed home.

As we boarded our return flight in Paris, I consoled my wife by observing, "You know, it's sort of scary how few snails you see in France."

The next ten months were the most difficult of my life. It was bad enough I had to concede that I had not heard God's voice clearly concerning spending a year in France—perhaps he had said, "Would you care to dance?" but my bruised ego would not let me resume life as usual.

I had made a big deal about stepping off the world for a year, and I was determined not to get back on. For the next several months I lived out the nightmare of every parent who sends his child off to get a higher education—that after he's finished, he won't be able to get a job. And along the way, I confirmed the prejudice of the hard-working, no-nonsense people in my hometown. "Them boys go off to college and they never do another decent day's work."

For ten months (except for a few systematic assaults on retreat centers) I sat around in one of the five local restaurants and pondered, contemplated, and wrote. I filled thick stacks of yellow legal pads with questions about "abundant-life," the "kingdom of heaven," and the human quest to return to Eden. It was only after the money from the sale of our possessions was completely exhausted that I gave up.

I put up a shingle and began a private practice. Even if I couldn't escort people to Eden, I could at least operate a lemonade stand on the roadside.

A Client Who Listens to Hermits

Buzzzt! The familiar sound of the phone-intercom let me know that my Friday client had arrived. "Send her in," I said, as I frantically scanned through the thick stack of notes.

My office door creaked open and a smiling head appeared in the narrow gap between door and wall. "Is this the right office?" the head asked.

"You are Diane?" I inquired.

"Yes, Diane Mershon," she said, looking relieved. Head and body quickly emerged from behind the door frame and walked in my direction with brisk strides.

"Then you're in the right place. Please sit down."

She thrust out a hand, gave me a firm handshake, and sank into an oversized blue sofa. Diane appeared to be in her early-to-mid forties. She had straight, dishpan blond hair that was beginning to be dusted with gray. Her eyes suggested more than a tinge of anxiety. They seemed to be on constant duty, scanning the environment with the detached vigilance of two security guards. She wore no makeup, but had a wholesome, Mennonite-type glow about her face. Her clothing—blue khaki pants, a long-sleeved cotton work-shirt, and her two-pairs-for-ten-dollars tennis shoes—and her gait, choppy and rigid produced a cloudy veneer that obscured her underlying femi-

ᴇ pen in her front pocket and the note-pad in her left
ᴇ evidence that she would be an eager client, and sug-
gestea ᴜiat she might be the type of individual who valued
function over form.

"What brings you to my office today, Diane?" I said, and
then inwardly winced, always wondering when some client
would say, "An '82 Buick. Why do you ask?" But Diane was a
serious-minded soul who was not in the habit of using humor
as a defense. It was 10 A.M., and she had already been up for six
hours, having driven more than two hundred miles to sit on
that sofa.

"Well I guess John Dobson's radio show is the main reason
I'm here."

"Excuse me? Do you mean James Dobson?" I asked.

"Oh, I guess. Well," she continued, "I was sitting in my living room about three weeks ago, just like I always do at 10:30
in the morning, after I've done all the morning chores and
David's schooling. He's my son, well, my natural son. I'm
homeschooling him and I was listening to Dobson's radio
show. A psychologist was being interviewed about his new
book, *Adrenaline and Stress* I believe it was called, and all of a
sudden he was describing my condition, these spells I've been
having for twenty-five years that no one has been able to diag-
nose, at least not to my satisfaction. He was describing my condition word-for-word. From the dizziness to the shortness of
breath he hit the nail head on. I just sat back and listened. I
couldn't believe it. So I wrote the Dobson folks and asked how
I could get in touch with this man. They gave me his address.

"You know him, of course, he teaches where you went to
school. So, I wrote him a fifteen-page letter explaining all that
I've been through with these spells. I asked him if he could
recommend someone I could speak to who was a Christian
psychologist and was familiar with his research. He wrote back

and said that I should contact you since you were nearer to me than any of his other former students. So, I guess I come here from my home town in South Carolina, by way of Southern California. Can you help me? I know you will need to hear more."

While I certainly would need to hear more, I had already heard enough to know that this case had real potential for helping me feel better about working on Fridays. I was just a few months into solo professional practice and it was already becoming clear that therapeutic "nuggets of wisdom" and "rules of thumb" were often more beneficial to have in the back of one's mind than knowledge of detailed techniques.

One of these "rules of thumb" was: *If the therapist is talking more than ten percent of the time, something is wrong.* I could safely predict that there would be no problem here! A second maxim was: *Even the best therapist cannot help a client who is not highly motivated.* Anyone who would drive two hundred miles, one-way, for therapy should score very high on any motivation test.

Diane's Family

Diane was very different from Bill, but she was also very similar. They both had experienced profound compassion deficits. They both had become addicted to the devil's narcotics at an early age.

During the following weeks she gave me a brief overview of her life. Diane was born to callous-handed parents who were part of a great migration that took place during the early to mid-1900s in the rural south. They packed up their strict work ethic and high tolerance for tedium and marched away from the family farm to the textile mill.

Her first six years of life were spent deep in a section of South Carolina where mules were made to pull plows through tired soil, chickens ran free in yards swept clean by stick-brooms, and the word "union" was seldom spoken. But her memories didn't start to pile up in any significant numbers until after her parents had packed themselves and their three children into a wood-paneled station wagon and headed north in search of a better life.

Her father found a job on an automotive assembly line turning bolts on carburetors, and her mother studied to be a nurse. Diane and her two older brothers settled into an elementary school where, to their dismay, their IQ had mysteriously dropped thirty points. It was apparently because the way they said "ice" sounded a lot like a slang word for donkey.

Diane, already somewhat of a loner, drifted even further away from her peers. If not for her tomboyish ways, which occasionally resulted in her brothers and their skinned-kneed friends tolerating her presence, the pain of her isolation would have been unbearable.

Diane's memories of her father were warm and tender. Yet, when she talked about him, there was a sadness in her eyes, a haunting sadness that on more than one occasion had caused the line from the poem by J.G. Whittier to drift through my mind, "of all the sad words of tongue and pen, the saddest are these: 'it might have been.'"

Evidently, her father was uncomfortable with any show of emotion, perhaps assuming it indicated weakness. He felt that the best way to demonstrate care was to be a provider, and he worked very hard at showing care. That is, he seldom turned down overtime pay.

The sentences Diane used to describe her father always followed a well-worn path from joy to lament. "I loved to play with him … when he had the time." "He was a lot of fun … well … that is … he could be." "I enjoyed being with him … but he was always on the go." Even with a loving, well-intentioned father, Diane suffered from a major deficit of fatherly love. He was rarely home physically. He was *never* home emotionally.

When, after scribbling several pages of notes about her father, I inquired about her mother, Diane's countenance underwent an unmistakable metamorphosis—from a childlike, wistful melancholia to subtle agitation.

Her head moved back to an erect position before she let a few clipped sentences escape. "She was a no-nonsense mother. She taught me practical things. She gave me what I needed." But like Diane's father, her mother did not give her what she needed most. As it turned out, Diane's mother was a prisoner of fear, and it kept her on a short chain. She was afraid to let Diane grow up, so she had her sleep in a crib until she was almost six. "I remember writing my letters on a piece of paper some mornings and calling out through the wooden bars for someone to come and look at what I had done."

She was afraid that Diane might become homosexual if she were touched or hugged by a female, so she avoided contact with her, always keeping her beyond arm's reach. She was afraid of Diane's maturing into a woman, so she ignored her developing breasts and told her nothing of menstruation. She was afraid of the anger that percolated in her own belly, so she kept her lips pursed against the pressure inside. She stuck out her jaw and furrowed her forehead in order to keep the anger from steaming out. Diane never knew for sure why her mother had so much wrath inside. But she assumed the blame, nonetheless. It made her feel dirty.

Diane's mother was a strict, religious woman. For decades she taught an orderly third-grade Sunday school class which she called the "Busy Bees." The more Diane talked about her mother, the more this seemed an appropriate name that symbolized a flurry of purposeful, practical activity by asexual drones, under the watchful eye of a queen.

Most of the kids at the churches Diane attended graduated

from that class after a year. The forty-six-year-old woman who sat in my office had never been promoted. She was still, very much, a busy bee.

Diane didn't marry until she was in her early thirties. In fact, she had seldom slowed down enough to date. She married a widower who had four children. "Those kids really needed a mother, and John needed someone to cook for him," she explained. It did seem a very practical thing to do. If it were viewed as a business partnership, the marriage was a success, but it was certainly uncluttered with affection. Their union did produce one of the only two sources of passion Diane had ever known, a biological son she named David.

Her other passion was for the vocation of nursing. During her late teens and early twenties she studied hard. "I wanted to be the best nurse I could be. I wanted to be able to know what the doctors were going to ask for before they even asked for it. I wanted the doctors to approve of me and say 'great job,' even if they only said it with their eyes."

Her enthusiasm for a career in nursing made her inability to function as a nurse all the more tragic. Soon after graduating as an RN, while she was scrubbing for a surgery, she became dizzy, began to sweat profusely, and developed shortness of breath. She ended up sitting on the cold tile floor of the lavatory area with her knees pulled tightly up to her chest.

After this experience, Diane became obsessed with the idea that the episode might repeat itself, at a dangerously inopportune time. The fear of this, coupled with repeated episodes of dizziness and hyperventilation, led to a gradual drifting away from her cherished career. At the time that she appeared in my office, she was working as an inspector in a windowless textile mill in her childhood hometown, a very long way from her cherished career.

These episodes or "spells" as she called them, had plagued

her sporadically the last twenty-five years of her life. Recently, they had begun to occur on a more frequent basis. She wanted answers, and so she had driven the two hundred miles to my office.

Diane's Number

Diane's number? 300.01, Panic Disorder without Agoraphobia (I finally memorized that book). But Diane didn't want to hear that. During the twenty-five years she had been experiencing these "spells," she had consulted with more than a dozen different physicians, representing a potpourri of specialization areas.

Physical disorders had been systematically ruled out. In fact, each of the last three physicians she saw scanned her thick stack of medical records and recommended a psychiatric consultation. She *certainly* didn't want to hear that.

With pricked ears Diane had listened to the words of Dobson's radio guest, Dr. Archibald Hart, as he described a link between adrenaline and stress. With white knuckles she grasped the non-psychiatric sounding explanation that adrenaline might play a role in her condition. Diane was right … sort of. Adrenaline does play a role in panic disorder.

Panic Attacks

To help my students get a feel for a panic attack I often ask them to imagine that a nine-hundred-pound saber-toothed tiger suddenly bounds through the classroom door, reducing it to splinters on hinges.

"Now watch the tiger as it bolts to the top of the table at the front of the room, turns, and crouches, muscles hardened into a ready-to-pounce position. It scans the room for a take-out lunch and makes eye contact with you. Saliva drips from its oversized incisors as it glares at you through cold, black eyes. It leaps at you ... but stops frozen in mid-air." I then ask, as the tiger remains in suspended animation, "What's happening in your body right now?"

"If the threat I described had been real," I continue, "or if your imagination were particularly vivid, some definite physiological changes would take place in your body. You would have rapid and shallow breathing, pounding heartbeat, trembling or shaking, sweating, flushes or chills, a drop in skin temperature in the hands and feet.

"That's the way your body prepares itself to fight or flee. That is the natural effect of fear on your body. It prepares you for confrontation or quick escape. And in this case your mind would wisely vote, run!"

For twenty-five years Diane had hundreds of unexpected encounters with "saber-toothed tigers" and with each confrontation, her body responded with full-blown panic. But when fear made Diane's heart race and her skin sweat, there were never any tigers present, not even a mangy cat. There were no consciously-known reasons to fight or to flee. But the occurrence of these attacks forced her to live with an additional fear, the fear that she could be "surprised" by an assault of terror at any given moment. This had driven her away from one of her only two passions in life, her career as a nurse, and too close to the other, her son, David.

The road from these recurring panic attacks back to her earlier compassion deficits was clearly marked and easy to follow. It was a multi-laned, interstate highway. Just by virtue of being human, Diane needed compassion and warm acceptance. But her childhood was more barren than the Sahara desert. It made perfect sense that she would look to others, particularly those in positions of authority, to provide her with the acceptance she craved. It made perfect sense that she would respond to anticipated rejection as one would respond to a tiger. Yet the question remained, why was she "surprised" by these fear responses? Why did they occur even when there was no apparent threat of rejection?

The well-lit highway between her present and her past had a lot of side roads. Some of those side roads were in dark, desolate places. The type of place where drug deals can go down.

Behavioral Narcotics

As a child, Diane could not bear to live in a world that was stalked by so many prowling tigers of rejection. That much fear was unbearable. So she, like most of us, became an easy victim of the invisible playground drug pusher with pockets filled with false solutions who lurks in the shadows of childhood.

He, a roaring feline in his own right, convinced her subconscious mind that relief from the pain of a love-starved heart was available … for a small price. He sold her drugs—three vials to be exact: one of perfectionism, one a mixture of avoidance and denial, and one filled with sublimation.

Each of these "drugs" gave her a measure of control over the unbearable pain of rejection. She was soon an addict to control. But the price she had to pay for these drugs was very high. It was the loss of hope for a real solution to her deathly fear of rejection. She also had to believe lies about the nature of God.

Perfectionism

Perfectionism has a long history. The Pharisees were heavy abusers, as are their modern-day descendants. And no wonder. It can be a powerful opiate, providing a hypnotic illusion of control. It can cause its user to feel free from the fear of rejection, since it all but legally mandates acceptance.

Diane, driven by a fear that she was somehow dirty and deserving of the tormenting pangs of fear of abandonment that churned inside, gulped down perfectionism for relief—devoting her time to activities that would ensure that she was "good enough" to be accepted. And it worked. Even when her perfectionist efforts at school, work, and play did not win the acceptance she craved, her head was so crowded with thoughts and plans of success that an overflow tumbled down and blocked the door to her heart. Better to be a busy bee than a lonely little girl, her subconscious must have reasoned. But just as prolonged use of stimulants can lead to a secondary dependence on barbiturates, Diane's use of perfectionism led to the use of other drugs—avoidance and denial.

Avoidance and Denial

Even our facade takes a lot of energy to keep shiny and polished. Sometimes it takes just too much energy. For those times, Diane found that other drugs were available, drugs which could cause such a distortion of perception that she was able to stare right at a fault and not even see it. Sometimes it was hard for me to keep the tears inside when Diane would talk so stoically about events in her life that would cause any non-drug user to scream in pain.

It was not at all uncommon for her to laugh out loud while describing painful rejection. Like the time a boy refused to kiss her and made a retching sound in his throat after the Coke bottle he had just set in motion stopped and pointed in her direction. But I believe the day she was the most stoned on denial was the day when she gave a dispassionate description of being sexually molested by her brother's friends (those same skinned-kneed friends) when she was ten.

"I guess I should tell you about this ... you hear so much about it nowadays ... I was afraid ... but I was more afraid they would stop letting me play with them if I ran away ... it wasn't that bad, really," she said with an eerie matter-of-factness. "They were just being boys."

The effects of these two drugs had caused an apparent atrophy of Diane's ability to label, and perhaps even to feel, emotions to the point that the only two adjectives I ever heard her use to describe a feeling were either "good" or "bad." The molestation? "Well, that made me feel bad."

"Not … angry, livid, helpless, bitter, violated, vengeful?" I inquired.

"No, I just felt bad."

Sublimation

The third vial was filled with what Freud called "sublimation." This emotional narcotic caused an intoxication that allowed Diane to somehow feel some of the nurture she craved for herself when she poured out nurture onto others. Undoubtedly, Freud would label her attraction to a nurturing profession, nursing, as a manifestation of sublimation. In the smothering love that she wrapped around her only biological son, David, she herself experienced the biggest high. At times the giving of love to her son caused her to temporarily forget the pain of her own compassion deficits. She gave out to David a magnified portion of what she so desperately needed to receive. The effort did not quench her thirst for compassion while it almost drowned her son.

Psychological Testing

As a clinical psychologist, I am often asked, "What's the difference between a psychologist and a psychiatrist?" To which I usually answer, "About twenty dollars an hour."

Of course, there are more important distinctions between these two mental health professions than billing rates, like their very distinct training models. The "medical model" is usually at the heart of training programs for psychiatrists. Their education is received through medical schools, in medical settings, and hence, they are well versed in the biological bases of behavior.

Psychiatrists remind all mental health professionals of an important anchor point—that at some level we are all a swirling universe of biochemical activity. Sometimes there is such a lack of chronicity within the skin-covered cosmos that correction is needed. Psychiatrists are the only mental health professionals who can prescribe pharmacological solutions.

Clinical psychologists are trained at universities through the "scientist-practitioner model." The ideals inherent in this model call for the education of a "scientist" (with skills in research methodology) who "practices" the craft of psychology in clinical settings.

It is the focus on research, the use of psychological testing, and the frequent dropping of phrases such as, "Is that supported in the literature?" which are distinctive of that mental health profession.

Naturally, as a psychologist, I would expect anything "hypothesized" about Diane's case to be confirmed through observation and, preferably, by test data. A test I routinely administered at the time I worked with Diane was the MMPI (Minnesota Multiphasic Personality Inventory), a brilliantly conceived test of personality dynamics, and in particular personality dysfunction.

To this day, in an updated version the MMPI remains the most widely used and researched objective personality inventory. If the diagnosis of "panic disorder" was correct; if Diane tended toward denial and avoidance; there should have been indications on the MMPI. But before we get to Diane's story, it may be helpful to imagine the following to get a grasp of how this test works.

Let's Construct a Test

Picture, if you will, a large indoor sports arena that has ten sections of seats emanating out from the central court like spokes on a bicycle wheel. Each section is filled by card-carrying members of ten different religious denominations. There is a section of Baptists, a section of Presbyterians, Catholics, Unitarians, and so forth. But, to be allowed to sit in one of the designated sections, one must be screened by a team of "denominational experts" who can unanimously agree that, "Yep, this person is through and through definitely a Baptist. And this one's a Presbyterian for sure."

An emcee appears at mid-court and announces to the crowd, "We are going to construct a test today, a test called the MMDPI (that's Minister's Mighty-fine Denominational Preference Indicator). I am going to read a long series of questions which can be answered either 'true' or 'false.' Your job is to respond with the answer that is correct for you. Are there any questions?" The "Baptist" section is awash with a sea of waving hands. "Good," says the emcee, "I just wanted to make sure you were all in the right sections.

"Now, let's proceed. Question number one: Do you sometimes jump over pews while you are worshipping? Question number two: Was John Calvin a good man? Number three: Do you have a visceral reaction to the image of a nun with a ruler?" and so forth. After more than a thousand questions have been asked and answered, the completed answer sheets are collected from each section and kept separate from the other sections' papers. The answer sheets are then run through a scantron. Any question answered in the same way by the majority of the members in a given section becomes an official MMDPI item.

That is, if most of the Pentecostals answered "false" to the question, "Do you brake for dispensationalists?" then that becomes an item on the "Pentecostal" scale and should help distinguish Pentecostals from the other nine denomination members. Any question that is not answered the same way by the majority of the members of a denomination cannot become an official item on that particular denominational scale. The end result is a 566-item test which contains ten pure "denominational" scales. The implications for church growth are, of course, obvious.

The real MMPI was formed in a similar fashion, except that instead of denominations, the focus was on 10 clinical conditions commonly found among mental health patients. The scales are: hypochondriasis, depression, hysteria, psychopathic deviate (authority conflicts), masculinity-femininity, paranoia, schizophrenia, hypomania, and social introversion.

In a similar fashion, if the majority of people in, let's say, the "depression" group responded "true" to the item, "my appetite is not as good as it used to be," then that becomes a depression scale item. The more depression scale items you endorse, the more likely it is that you are depressed, and if you are not, you are answering important questions in a similar fashion to a large group of depressed people.

The results of Diane's MMPI testing were very supportive of my diagnostic impressions. They offered objective backing for the presence of personality characteristics which would suggest: denial of emotional pain, repressed anger for authority figures, over-controlled anxiety, and perfectionism.

Further testing with the Rorschach (the classic ink blot test) and a sentence completion test, echoed the suggestions of the interview and MMPI data. If she weren't experiencing a panic disorder, if she were not a heavy user of perfectionism, denial, and sublimation, then the Pope isn't Catholic.

Treatment by the Book

By the time I began to work with Diane, a definite pattern had emerged in my approach to psychotherapy, which I followed with the vast majority of my clients. It was almost identical to the approach I had taken with Bill.

1. As a rule I spend the first one or two sessions conducting a structured clinical interview. This interview is not terminated until an accurate diagnosis has been established (even if the diagnosis is "no diagnosis," which, given insurance restrictions, can be the most difficult one to write down) and a detailed treatment plan has been outlined.

2. During the next four to six sessions I usually have the client go through a "history of memories" experience. This involves having a patient spend approximately thirty minutes per day in solitude, jotting down memories that come back, while focusing on different periods of his life (e.g., the elementary school years).

This is an Adlerian-type exercise based on the assumption that, given a field of thousands of possible memories, the particular ones that come to a client do so because of some relevance.

Even if this were not the case, I would still use this exercise for several other purposes:

- "catching-up" on the client's life in the briefest possible time;
- continuing to establish rapport;
- earning the right (through being a compassionate and patient observer) to offer possible insights; and
- to afford observations concerning the client's level of insight and judgment and to allow *him* to "be in the driver's seat" concerning his own therapy (always the preferred scenario).

3. I then target the most pressing problem area the client is experiencing and help him develop and carry out a change strategy which should bring relief. In Diane's case the choice of a change strategy was a simple one. What the literature said was clear. Systematic desensitization, a behavioral therapy technique of counter-conditioning, was and is the treatment of choice for panic attacks.

Systematic desensitization is based, albeit not by design, on a scriptural teaching—"perfect love casts out all fear." Fear and love are physiological opposites. The body cannot simultaneously experience a fear response (shallow breathing, rapid heartbeat, cold, and clammy palms) and a love-relaxation response (deep breathing, slow, steady heartbeat, and warm hands). One cancels out the other.

So, Diane was taught several types of relaxation exercises and asked to practice these exercises twice a day until she was able to experience a deep relaxation response.

Together we constructed a hierarchy of anxiety-producing events (we used actual episodes from her work that often had preceded an anxiety attack). We then went through a counter-conditioning process in systematic desensitization in which she would imagine herself engaging in the events at the "less threatening end" of the hierarchy, while maintaining a state of physical relaxation. She then transferred the counter-conditioning from an imagined situation to the *in vivo* (real life) experience.

In theory, this procedure breaks the connection between anxiety-producing situations and the onset of a fear response. In real life ... it worked! After fifteen to eighteen sessions, Diane experienced a significant drop in the number of panic attacks she was experiencing.

She was elated. I was elated. But, we both openly wondered about the role that Jesus as "Prince of Peace" might play in her life.

A Few Leaps with the Hermit

No doubt about it, Diane had learned to better control her fear response. She had also learned a great deal about the underlying dynamics which caused her to be surprised by these reactions. The invisible tigers were coming out of hiding. But as with Bill, there was a gnawing tiger in my own gut. I felt that a lot more could be done to help Diane.

After all, I wasn't convinced that systematic desensitization and insight-oriented psychotherapy was what Jesus had in mind when he said to his disciples, "The Counselor, the Holy Spirit, whom the Father will send in my name will teach you all things and will remind you of everything I have said to you. Peace I leave with you; my peace I give you. I do not give to you as the world gives. Do not let your hearts be troubled and do not be afraid" (John 14: 26-27 NIV).

I was equally unconvinced, however, that sermonette psychotherapy was what he had in mind. Even in the middle of the afterglow of our successful work, I began to see Diane as I had seen Bill and Adam, still sitting in a rowboat, adrift and lonely in the middle of a vast sea.

Certainly, it was profound compassion deficits that had set Diane in motion, feverishly "rowing" in search of acceptance. She had lived her life searching to find a "home," a place where love and favor were freely given. But she had come to believe that "earnership"—being the best that she could be— was the only way to get there.

She didn't come to see me, however, because of the compassion deficits or because of the "drugs." She came because something was interfering with the rowing. This something was the fact that she never knew when she would be surprised by panic—a natural response to a shout from deep within her subconscious that said, "NO MATTER WHAT YOU DO, IT WON'T BE GOOD ENOUGH ... YOU WILL BE FOUND

OUT AND REJECTED ... YOUR ANGER, YOUR SEXU-
AL IMPULSES WILL BE EXPOSED ... YOU ARE
WORTHLESS!"

No doubt about it, I had been able to help Diane. I had
helped her to go back to her rowing without having to worry
so much about those bothersome interruptions of panic. But I
was about to close her file for the last time with her still adrift
and a long, long way from home. Fortunately, about this time
we bumped right smack into the hermit.

Diane: "I can't tell you how much I appreciate what you have
        done for me. It was surely worth the drive to find a
        Christian psychologist. You always respected my
        Christianity. You never made fun of it or tried to take it
        away; that was very important to me. But you knew
        how to teach me the right techniques, too. With my
        training as a nurse, for you to know your profession
        and make the right prescriptions, well, it just had to be.
        Anyway, I want you to know that I feel like a new per-
        son."

Me: "So, you're feeling pleased with the progress you've
        made. And it sounds like we may be getting pretty
        close to the end of our time together. What do you
        think?"

Diane: "Yeah, I think I should be trying this on my own for
        awhile. I may want to call and come back from time-
        to-time for, uh, booster shots or something. If that's
        OK? I have got a question, though. My pastor asked
        me this when I told him about the wonderful changes
        that are happening for me. He asked me how Jesus, as
        "the Prince of Peace," had been part of my help. I
        don't know how you feel about this, but I told him
        that he led me to you. He loved me enough to help
        me find someone who could figure out what I needed

to do. That was his role. Right? (long pause) Is that the way you see it?"

Me: "Well, you are very gracious. And to tell the truth, I'm not sure I've got a good answer for you. I believe that there is a real Prince of Peace, and that he lives in an invisible, upside-down kingdom, a kingdom that spreads out all around us and inside us. But I'm not sure that many people enjoy all of the benefits of life in that kingdom. I'm not sure many people live there. I think that in order to enjoy the benefits of it, we have to really live in his kingdom and it has to become more real to us than (I knock on the leg of my chair) this tangible world. I can't say that, uh, in our work together, we ever entered into the kingdom where he reigns as prince. What do you think?"

Diane looked at me with wide eyes.

Oops, I thought, but it was too late. With that comment our work together would take an abrupt turn. We were about to go, in the words of C. S. Lewis, in a direction that would take us "further up and further in."

"Would you help me find that kingdom?" she asked. Before you could say malpractice suit, I had agreed. Psychotherapy was about to become spiritual direction. The ephemeral world would start to come into clear focus, framed by a blur of the tangible. I felt a lot like Luke Skywalker must have felt the first time he made a jump to light speed maneuver, as we shot past most all of my previous conceptions about psychotherapy as if they were stationary stars. It was a great ride while it lasted.

Then we hit an asteroid. The first thing we discovered, during our journey into spiritual direction, was that in this new arena, Diane had a different set of presenting problems. Despite forty-plus years of church attendance, she had never been introduced to the idea that the kingdom of heaven is not only by-and-by, but also here-and-now. That was a major problem for someone who wanted the scriptural promises about life in the kingdom applied to her, in the nasty here-and-now.

It was also a major problem that she felt completely unworthy of the love of a royal, heavenly Father. And it was certainly a problem that she could not believe that he wanted to talk to her. And even if she could have mustered belief, she had no idea how to discern between his voice and her own thoughts or between his voice and the voice of his arch enemy. Those are real problems for anyone who needs to be able to rest in secure love. And since there is nothing constant and dependable except the kingdom of God, I guess they could be real problems for us all.

Reality of the Kingdom

At first I thought it would be a good idea to begin with the concept of practicing the presence of God—the discipline of hanging-out with the Divine. We began by reading and discussing the devotional classic, *The Practice of the Presence*, by Brother Lawrence. However, it soon became evident that this idea was premature.

Diane wasn't really convinced that God and his kingdom were available to her. She had seen too much corruption in the tangible church to believe in something so pristine. So, we backed up and began with Plato's Cave.

"Diane, have you ever heard the story Plato told, a few millennia ago, about an underground cave?" She shook her head.

"Well, let me tell it to you, at least what I can remember."

I told her the story I told you at the beginning of this book and when I had finished, I could tell by the tears sliding down Diane's cheek that she understood why I had shared it with her.

Before I could speak, she said, "You really do believe in this invisible, upside-down kingdom, don't you?" She didn't need my answer. "You think that is what Jesus was talking about. You think they put him to death because they couldn't grasp the realness of the world he knew about."

"Yeah, I'm afraid I do. And even worse, I think that he is waiting to help all who will follow him to find their way up and outside our world of shadows and into his real kingdom."

"The invisible one that's all around us and inside us?" she said with a sly smile.

"Yeah, that one."

But then she added, "What about the church? Is it in the cave too?"

"I don't know about the church." (Although I had my suspicions that any given congregation might be anywhere from still bound and tied, to free yet still in the cave, to outside playing in the garden.) "But, I'm curious about you. Where do you see yourself?"

She spent the next several sessions answering that question. During the weeks that followed, the world outside the cave became very real to Diane. She truly began to believe that the kingdom of heaven existed all around her, and that it was ruled by a King, a Prince of Peace, and an invisible Counselor.

But a problem remained. She could not make herself believe that she deserved to leave the cave and play in the fields of God. "Surely, I have to earn the right to go out and play." That reasoning kept her both chained and yearning. Then another story came to mind. I think it was probably sent from outside the cave.

Buying God's Love for a Quarter

"Diane, I want you to imagine something. I want you to imagine that your son, David ... he's four, right ... notices, by observing his parents, that money is something pretty important. He sees that it is used to pay bills, buy groceries, and that amazingly, it can even be exchanged for ice cream. It dawns on him that if he can earn some of this valuable stuff, he'll be a better son and make you and his dad happy.

"So David gets up early one morning and toddles off to the local sewing plant. He applies for a job there. The manager tells David that there isn't much a four-year-old can do. But, being a shrewd manager with an eye for the bottom line, he tells David that if he will walk around and pick up scraps of cloth and put them in the trash, he'll give him 'a big shiny' piece of money—twenty-five cents, for eight hours work in a hot sewing plant.

"David is elated that he has a job and that he can contribute to the family. He works all day. At the end of the day he walks home, dragging his tired feet. He comes up to you, and with a sweat- and dirt-streaked hand he holds out a quarter and says, 'Here you are, Mommy, I hope this will make you love me more.' You are, of course, in a state of shock. You have missed your son all day. You don't know what is happening. And you surely don't need his quarter. But David will not be reasoned with.

"The next day he gets up before dawn. He has decided that if one quarter is good, two are better. He walks back to the mill and asks the manager if he can start working two shifts. The manager quickly agrees.

"For the next few weeks David works sixteen hours a day at the sewing plant. And each evening he drags himself home, face dirty and clothes wet from sweat, and says with a tired whisper, 'Here's two more. I hope you love me for them. I'm really trying to be a good boy.'

"So Diane, what do you think?"

"I think that is the worst story I have ever heard! I think I want to cry." She already was.

"It wouldn't make you happy to be getting all that money?" If Diane had ever allowed herself to curse, it would have been then. But she satisfied herself with a resounding eighty-decibel "Umph!"

"Well," I went on, trying to seem innocent, "how could your son have made you happy?"

"He could hear what I was trying to say to him! He could have quit that stupid job that I never wanted him to do and go out in the back yard and laugh and play like a kid! That would have made me ecstatic."

"Exactly, Diane. And I think your Father would like for you to quit doing all the work he never asked you to do. He doesn't need the quarters anyway, he can turn stones into gold if he needs the cash. He wants you to go out and play with him. There is something you could do for him. You could throw your head back and laugh like a kid—a kid who trusts him with a simple childlike faith."

Diane started crying pretty hard. I think our second presenting problem (thinking she must earn the right to play) was developing a large crack. She was about to start believing that God didn't need or want her quarters. He wanted her.

Practice His Presence, Hear His Voice

Over the next few weeks Diane let herself relax more and more into the truth she had found in that story. She was sinking into the pleasant realization that there really was a kingdom of peace and joy, and that the king was a loving Father who wanted her to come out of her cave and play with him in his real world.

But there was one more problem. Diane summarized it with one of her questions. "I actually believe that God wants to spend time with me and talk with me. But when I spend time with him, how do I know that it is his voice I am hearing—

inside my head. (You don't have to worry about my having hallucinations.) How do I know what I am hearing is not just my own thoughts nor is it the voice of Satan?"

Oh boy! This sure wasn't Kansas anymore, and I was no wizard. I was just an "at-least-for-now" licensed psychologist, a long way from home.

"Well, Diane … " I went for broke. I told her about how I was trying to make that distinction in my own prayer life. Specifically, I told her about a seminar my wife and I attended in Titusville, Florida, with Reverend Peter Lord.[2]

Pastor Lord had shared some powerful insights about knowing the voice of God in prayer, or to use his words, "How you know you are listening to station WGOD, instead of WSIN." It's really pretty simple in a profound sort of way. Peter Lord's insights were very helpful to Diane as she tried to discern the voice of the only stable source of acceptance in the universe from those that seemed to either enjoy or perpetuate her pain.

For the most part, the idea was to be aware of your emotions after "hearing the communication."

If you felt "driven," "guilty," "anxious," "fearful," or "condemned," the chances were pretty great that you had heard from WSIN. However, if you felt "invited," "peaceful," "calm," "loved," or perhaps "gently convicted," it was more likely that you were hearing from God. The process also involved asking yourself certain questions, like, "If God is described as a gentle shepherd in Scripture, why would he start acting like a cattle driver?"

Having already spent considerable time walking with Diane through her childhood memories, it was relatively easy to spot thoughts which were part of the collection of "tapes" from her past. It was amazing to see the benefit to Diane when she made the discovery that she had spent most of her adult life burdened by guilt and self-condemnation as a result of thoughts from the devil that she had been falsely attributing to God.

"I wondered why a loving Father-God would be saying stuff like, 'If you don't do this or that, something bad will happen to David.' It just never seemed to fit. But I drove myself to do whatever I thought he said." On more than one occasion I recalled the words of Peter Lord, "Most people who are busy doing what they think is God's business, heard their inspiration from the devil."

It took several months and a whole anthology of stories, but eventually Diane was in the boat with the "hermit." She believed in him. She believed in his invisible kingdom and that he wanted to spend time with her. She even believed that he wanted to talk with her, and be her personal, twenty-four-hour-a-day Counselor. I believe it was really happening.

"You know," Diane said at the start of one of our sessions, "it seems like God surely is repeating himself a lot when he talks to me."

"What are the themes?" I asked.

"Over-and-over, I'm hearing, 'Diane, you're my precious child. I will always love you; and I will never leave you. Let go. Fall back into my arms. Let go.' What do you make of that?"

"I think that maybe you're being invited to take your oars out of the water."

"But what does that mean?" she asked.

"I really don't know. Maybe it has something to do with allowing the creedal statement, 'Jesus is Lord (and I ain't),' to have a new depth of meaning for you."

Diane was very brave. She took her oars out of the water and bathed in the warmth of a calm, irradiating trust. All of the significant people in her life saw the visible changes at the surface of her life, as perfect love slowly pushed out imperfect fear from her core.

I'm sure it was no coincidence that her panic attacks did not return, even without the aid of anti-anxiety medication or relaxation exercises. She was experiencing the perfect peace that is not from this world.

Unfortunately, there was still a "sea monster" to deal with. And it made itself known with an almost audible shriek as it suddenly erupted into view. Diane had been doing great for several months. My biggest problem with her case was the guilt I was feeling about billing for spiritual direction.

A Major Detour

Unfortunately, Diane was doing so well that her friends, relatives, and family must have simultaneously arrived at the conclusion that she was now strong enough to handle some of the advice and criticism that they had been keeping from her because of the "spells." They assumed, I guess, that a stronger Diane could benefit from their suggestions. So, they let them fly.

There was a definite theme to the barrage of advice. "You know you're smothering David." "What do you think your step-children think about the 'special' relationship the two of you have? You've got to let him go."

They were right. Diane *was* overly protective of David. In fact, she made an infant of him, just as she had been made an infant as a child. She rarely let him out of her sight. It often sounded as if she would have a tissue under his nose for weeks before his first winter cold. And the special love she felt for him went unconcealed in front of his brothers and sisters.

Their diagnosis of Diane's behavior was accurate. However, the timing of their "treatment plan" was way off. Then a voice inside Diane's head, one that did not belong to her or the Prince of Peace began to say, "Remember what I have been saying about letting go? You must let go of David ... Now!"

Diane was not able to muster the faith to believe that this sea monster was an illusion or that it would pass through her like an X-ray if she would refuse to give it substance. Instead, she felt its scaly hand crash down upon her. David was an idol to Diane. He was an "Isaac" that she would need to be willing to leave on an altar at some point. But she was not hearing that message from God.

It has been my experience that the Great Physician gently unwraps our wounds, one layer of gauze at a time, slowly bringing the tender surface in contact with healing air and light. Diane's bandages were being ripped off, tearing scabs and opening sores. My talks with Diane about discerning God's voice, my reminders to her about the nature of the Gentle Shepherd fell on deaf ears. She was too frightened to stare the sea monster into oblivion.

But then a way out appeared for Diane. Her pastor showed her a way to escape from her fears. He told her that she should seriously question any psychologist who was trying to do the work of a minister.[3] He told her that this concept of letting go had a decidedly eastern ring to it, and that maybe she would be better off if she would just forget the whole, weird experience. "I serve a God that says, 'hold on,' not one that says 'let go,'" he said, not realizing he was trying to smother a fire with gasoline. He gave her a way out.

When she started rowing again, the tormenting voice stopped, and the sea monster went back under water, its work accomplished. When her family saw the return of her frailty, they quit making their suggestions. Diane called and scheduled a farewell session. It was the saddest and the strangest session I have ever experienced.

She recalled all of her good work with the desensitization. She recalled her experience with the kingdom and with the King. She confessed a great confusion as to how something that made her feel like a prodigal child in the arms of a loving Father could be wrong for her. But she was convinced that the words of her pastor were correct. There was nothing I could say or do. She had found a way to have a "measure" of God while keeping the control of her life in her own hands.

I guess that's what all false religions provide. I guess that road is always the last major detour off the narrow path back to Eden. A firm handshake, a moist look, and our final session was over. "I'm sorry I couldn't stay for the whole hour," she explained from the hallway. "I've got to hurry home so I can do homeschooling with David before the other kids get home."

"I hope she doesn't get stuck behind a chicken truck," I thought to myself, "or it could take forever to get back home."

6

Hummingbirds and Light Switches

So many come—for spiritual advice
or ghostly counsel, as they say;
they speak of pain and loss,
confusion and despair, fear and death,
All I did was listen.

For I believe full surely
that God's Spirit is in us all,
giving light, wisdom, understanding
speaking words in us
when we cannot speak,

showing us gently what we would not see,
what we are afraid to see,
so we may show pity, mercy, forgiveness,
to ourselves.

Julian of Norwich

I always imagined myself to be a teacher. When my first grade friends wanted to grow up to be cowboys and firemen or some creative combination of the two, I just wanted to teach first grade. When their horizons expanded and they decided that the work of astronauts and oceanographers was more to their liking, I had decided that I would like the work of a junior high school teacher.

And when they settled for careers as bankers, dentists, and lawyers, it was still settled in my mind. I wanted to be a teacher. So it only surprised my banker friends when I gave up a bustling clinical practice for chalk, transparencies, and a captive audience of soon-to-be-professional counselors.

From the first day of private practice I suspected that I was in trouble; I kept having to repress the urge to wheel in a chalkboard and talk from behind a podium. But, it was when the desire hit me to assign mid-term grades and put a few clients on "therapeutic probation" that I knew it was time to move on. And move on we did. We moved far away from our beloved rural Georgia to one of the world's largest suburbs-by-the-sea, to teach at a private Christian graduate school.

Our new environment of cul-de-sacs and drive-through fried chicken took some getting used to. There was more asphalt than vegetation, more sea gulls than robins, and more city buses than chicken trucks. It wasn't all bad!

In the suburbs we had to adjust to a whole new way of doing things, like measuring distance. "How far to the public library?" "Well that would be three shopping strips and a mall from here. But don't go past a Taco Bell or you've gone too far."

All-in-all, going from small town life to suburbia was depressing. It was like eating a cold can of Chef Boyardee spaghetti when you are used to homemade spaghetti. You just knew that what you were forcing down was a bland imitation.

But some things remained the same regardless of population density. People remained the same. They still experienced painful compassion deficits. They still tried to ease the suffering with strong emotional and behavioral "narcotics." And, like their country-cousins, they were composed of two selves, one false and one true. I knew this because I still maintained a small private practice on the side. I knew this because of Janet Weston.

Another Time, Another Sailor

Janet appeared in my office one April afternoon. She glided across the room barely touching sole to carpet. Her head was covered with thick auburn hair that remained in motion for a moment after she had been seated. Her skin was Irish-white; her features frail and angular. She had large brown cow eyes and a youthful appearance. She looked much more like a wide-eyed child than a thirty-five-year-old mother. And she was here because she had been scarred by years of abuse.

I asked the usual question, "Where would you like to start?" She answered by filling the room with words. In the ensuing weeks it became distressingly obvious that her eyes, which looked so open and naive, had witnessed more pain than anyone should have to see in a dozen lifetimes.

"I'm really not sure why I'm here or if I should be here," she began. "It's just that a few days ago, at work, one of my bosses—this is very hard to talk about—put his arm around my waist while standing next to me in my office. I know he didn't mean anything by it, but before he had time to blink, I had slapped his hand away and, quite literally, found myself on the other side of the room from him. I had knocked over my trash can and caused him to spill coffee all over his suit ... I think it was a new one, too ... in the process. He said, 'What the hell is the matter with you?' And I just looked at him from a distance with my heart pounding in my throat, and said, 'I don't know. I really don't know.' Over and over I said it. Finally he said, 'Well, I don't know either. And I'm sorry if I offended you,' and he left the room. I'll never forget the puzzled look on his face."

I was, of course, wondering if she had felt sexually harassed by the incident, and if this was a common occurrence at work.

But before I could turn my thoughts into a question, she volunteered, "I can't even make myself feel better by saying that he deserved my reaction. It wasn't like he had been harassing me. He's not like that at all. He's a kind grandfatherly type, the type that leaves the room at the first hint of an off-color story. I know he didn't mean anything by it, except to say, 'Good work. I'm proud of you.' And that's why I'm here. My reaction was way out of proportion to what he did and I don't know where it came from."

I said nothing for a few seconds, waiting to see if she wanted to say more. I broke the silence with, "So your reaction not only surprised your boss, it surprised you as well?"

"Yes, it really shocked me. But, now that I'm here, I feel like I'm just taking up your time, and somebody else's time who deserves to be here." She was rising from her chair as she spoke.

"No, Janet," I reassured, "this is your time, and I'm delighted to be here with you."

The rest of the hour was quickly spent as Janet talked more about the incident at work and several other times in which she had been surprised by her reactions (usually fearful or angry) to people. She also made references to troubling emotions of depression and anxiety, and to her too-busy schedule.

While she talked, my attention was occasionally drawn away by the brilliant, glittering colors of a hummingbird as it hovered around a flowering bush just outside my window. Perhaps I should have paid a little more attention to the bird. In many ways it was a metaphor for Janet's life; a metaphor that she did not yet understand.

Janet was extremely insecure and suffering from a very poor self-concept. She lived with the persistent fear that any happiness she felt would be ripped away. She stayed in a constant, whirling flight in an attempt to out-maneuver her despair as she searched for the nectar of compassion.

Perhaps Jung would have assessed that Janet was suffering from an "insecurity complex." Perhaps Rogers would have decided that she was a textbook case representing the need for "self-actualization." And, it is very likely that in today's zeitgeist she would be referred to as having all the makings of a codependent personality. But regardless of how the results of compassion deficits are rearranged, repackaged, and re-labeled, Janet showed enough symptoms of love abuse to justify a whole catalogue of classifications.

Janet's Family

Janet's father was dead. He died of a ruptured aorta when she was only eight years old. She never shed a tear. She remembered him as a short, powerfully-built man who worked, when it suited him, as a longshoreman.

By her descriptions, he was a human capacitor for anger, storing it up throughout the workday. At night, with the help of a fifth of cheap whisky, he invariably discharged his lightning bolts of rage onto his wife, his son, and Janet.

Janet had two distinct groupings of memory concerning her father. She called one of these categories "the bright-angry ones." These included many fiery-flashes of him, a drunken demon, rampaging through their tiny house, his face beet red and twisted by hate. In those memories, she saw him as a bellowing tyrant who snorted out threats, upended furniture, and smashed dishes on dining room walls, and on her mother's back.

In these memories she always saw her mother scurrying to

escape; usually ending up behind a locked door. Her father would eventually tire of pounding his fist against wood. It was then that she was most vulnerable. It was then that he invariably turned his attention elsewhere, directing his evil glare around the room until it fell, usually, upon her.

It was a look that caused her to become rigid with fright, like an animal surprised by approaching headlights. From there, the bright, flashing memories went no further.

Unfortunately, there was another distinct category of memories, dark, spotty images which she had long hoped were nothing more than ghastly nightmares. But they were very real. They were shadowy recollections of her father in her bed, his breath smelling of whisky, his hands treating her like his wife instead of a frightened little girl.

But that was her secret. That was why she had never shed a tear when he died. And that was the main reason a pat on the back had sent her scurrying across her boss's office.

Janet's mother didn't provide much consolation. She was a weak and helpless woman who failed to protect her daughter. That was understandable. What was not understandable was why she also failed to provide the warm love and acceptance which might have diluted Janet's shame. Instead of gentle caresses, Janet remembered the sting of harsh slaps; and instead of words of absolution, she remembered words of blame for her father's perversions.

"You shouldn't look at him the way you do, Janet! You should sit more like a lady and he wouldn't bother you!"

It seemed to Janet that almost everyone who reached out to her, when she was a child, either wanted to hit her or to take something precious away. It became very difficult for her to trust emotions such as happiness, and very easy for her to expect pain.

Janet was able to find some solace during her childhood. She found it at church and school.

She had wonderful memories of a few special teachers who showed her kindness. Warm smiles, pats on the hand, her name remembered, her colored pictures prominently displayed on the bulletin board. What for most would be mere table-scraps of compassion were for Janet seven-course meals. She gobbled them up and began to live for these "meals." She began to "perform" to receive more of this sustenance for emotional life. Her metamorphosis into a "hummingbird" had begun.

Her most cherished childhood memory was when a church decided to adopt her family one Christmas. At age thirty-five, her eyes still welled with tears when she remembered the sight of three "fancy-dressed, perfume-smelling" ladies standing in the doorway of her childhood home, like radiant fairy-god-mothers from a far away land. In their arms were brightly-wrapped presents and bags of food.

She told me how they deposited their gifts under what had been a barren Christmas tree, filling the whole room with the scent of Chanel No. 5 and the magic of Christmas.

They went back to their car and returned with a huge turkey and a whole grocery bag of candy. It took her years to figure out why the three ladies were all mopping their cheeks with the sleeves of their wool coats as they filed out the front door.

By that time Janet had already begun to look beyond her parents to find the acceptance and recognition she craved. And that incredible act of Christmas kindness confirmed to her that she was on the right course. If she were to survive, she must look outside the peeling, tar-paper-covered walls of her home.

Her transformation into a "hummingbird" continued. As she found kindness and acknowledgment from surrogate parents, usually teachers and ministers, her life increasingly became a feverish whir of people-pleasing activity. The attention this brought, the nectar of human recognition, is what began to sustain her emotional life.

Without it she would have died. With her constant craving for it, however, her life was the life of an addict. She couldn't even imagine what it would feel like to still her wings and rest on the petals.

By the time Janet entered my office she had spent more than twenty-five years in an exhausting pursuit of this nectar. Pastors, teachers, and bosses. These were her "flowers." But she was discovering that with flowers there are bees; and she was also discovering that her arms were not designed to keep her aloft.

Psychological Testing

As part of the counseling process Janet filled out the MMPI and several other paper-and-pencil measures of personality and emotion. The results of these tests were very consistent with her own descriptions and recollections.

The "Validity Scales" of the MMPI suggested that she was being unusually open and forthright in her responses, perhaps using the test as a forum to cry out for help. That is, she was now exceptionally free to admit to pain—emotional and physical—and to admit many unusual life experiences, things that she had kept hidden away for years. Apparently, she hoped that the admissions would be a signal-flare for help.

The results of the testing were also highly consistent with her own reports suggesting that she was an individual who was experiencing very high levels of anxiety, fear, and depression, but not high enough to suggest the need for hospitalization. Her test scores further indicated that she was a very creative, artistic person, prone to use her fantasy life as an escape from emotional pain.

It wasn't surprising that the results indicated that she was an individual with a history of "some kind of rejecting or devaluing situation," nor was it a shock to read that those who score like Janet often wrestle with depression, anxiety, worry, guilt, multiple fears, apprehension, and morbid ruminations over the course of their entire lifetime—at least when their wings get tired.

Additional Formulations and Traditional Therapy

After several weeks of additional history taking, focused exploration, and additional psychological testing, there was no obvious diagnosis (*DSM*) for Janet's condition. It was apparent that her long-standing feelings of insecurity, fear, anxiety, and mildly persistent depression had increased in intensity since the incident at work, perhaps suggesting the diagnosis of 309.28: Adjustment Disorder with Mixed Emotional Features. However, even if her emotional state returned to what was "normal," for her it would still be a painful way to live—fearful, distrusting of happiness, addicted to attention that could be won from authority figures—an emotional prisoner of past abuse.

Even before Janet first walked into my office, I had become a psychologist holding with a loose grip the theories and techniques offered by the discipline of psychology. While I had great respect for Rogers, Skinner, Ellis, Freud, Jung, and the like, I had come to view them more as brilliant (I could not even see the summit of their intelligence from my low-lying position on the normal curve), but blindfolded explorers who had discovered an elephant (the psyche) by latching onto its various extremities (feelings, behaviors, thoughts, or dimly-viewed subconscious motivations).

Unfortunately, most of them had become famous by loudly lobbying that the extremity was the elephant. In my mind, psychotherapy, which literally means "soul-healing," had lost any focus on the soul. This was very bad news for the soul-sick. Along with these thoughts, a gnawing fear had been growing in my gut for a number of years. *What if the psychological techniques I have been using accomplish little more than scraping off benign, surface-level skin cancers, while leaving huge malignant masses to grow unchecked beneath the surface, slowly destroying all that truly is the elephant?*

Along with Hamlet, I knew that there are more things in heaven and earth than are dreamt of in our philosophies (or all our psychology). I also knew that the cancer inside Janet, which went undetected by rigorous application of the *DSM* was fear. There was a deep, dark fear that the way her parents treated her was the way she deserved to be treated; a fear that she did not merit happiness, security, or acceptance; a fear that she really could not trust anyone, even the Supreme Love-Giver.

I knew that her fear was born out of the extreme compassion deficits (and compassion injuries) she had suffered as a child. She was treating the pain it produced with "narcotics"—small doses of denial and a huge ingestion of recognition and acceptance from substitute parents (teachers, preachers, and bosses). I further suspected that her "false self" held tightly to a hummingbird-like approach to securing "nectar," while her "true self" sat emaciated and imprisoned, far away from its rightful place on the throne of her life. Her "true self" needed to be liberated. Her paralyzing fear needed to be irradiated with the healing beams of God's love.

I was enough of a believer in the scientist-practitioner model of clinical psychology to feel guilty about suggesting an intervention strategy for which there was little support in the literature. I felt a professional and ethical obligation to go with the mainstream and practice that I had been taught. So, I went with what had been written in the logs of the first three helpers. Relaxation training was prescribed for her anxiety. Assertion training, with heavy doses of role-play and modeling, was used in working with her on issues of her insecurity.

I taught her some techniques to aid against her depression—pleasant events scheduling (doing more fun stuff each day) and cognitive restructuring (putting new records in our mental juke box, and breaking some of the old ones). Additionally, we conducted many sessions of support and free explorations toward the end of finding insight concerning her idealization of authority figures. We worked together for a little over six months and both of us were reasonably satisfied with her progress. I had begun to talk about termination. It was about then that the hermit appeared.

The Hermit

Ten to fifteen minutes into our twenty-fifth session, I was allowing small talk to continue because I dreaded bringing the focus back to termination.

Janet: "Did you know that my favorite animal is the hummingbird?"

Me: "No, I didn't know that. How come?" I asked, wondering if she had caught me staring out the window at my feathered friend.

Janet: "They're just so beautiful. You know, they're so bright and colorful. And they're such hard workers—wings a blur, hovering around flowers. I don't know if they even sleep at night."

Me: "So, hummingbirds are your favorite animal ... because of their beauty and their work ethic."

Janet: "Yeah, but it's really more of an emotional thing. I just like them because I like them. I can get lost in time watching them. *Really*. I lose track of time staring at them. I think I identify with them somehow."

Me: "You feel like you live a hummingbird's life in some ways?"

Janet: "Oh yeah. If God had made me an animal, I am sure it would have been a hummingbird."

Me: "How do you feel like a hummingbird, right now?"

Janet: "Well, it's not the beautiful part—except maybe for the way I dress. It's more the blur of the wings, the busyness. I'm always on the go, always looking for something, never able to rest."

Me: "Always searching for something you don't have? Always on the go? Exhausted?"

Janet: "Yea. And I can never quite find it, or I can't ever get enough of it to last. It's like being hungry but never able to feel full. Like you are starving and can only eat shadows."

Me: "Yeah, I think I've had a nightmare like that. It sounds exhausting and incredibly frustrating. Has our time together given you any ideas about what it is that you are searching for?"

Janet: "Oh, yes. I'm looking for love, the love I never had as a child. I'm looking for affirmation, 'atta-boys,' and pats on the back. I'm looking for security."

Me: "But you never feel full, no matter how much 'nectar' you find, and pats on the back can still send you scurrying across the room. This may seem like an odd question, but do you relate to God in hummingbird ways?"

Janet: "Well, I sure buzz around the church like one. I think I'm on every committee they have. I teach a Sunday school class. I pretty much turn the lights on and off over there."

Me: "Have you found what you are searching for there?"

Janet: "Yes and no. I find it, but it doesn't last. I can never seem to relax into it. I don't trust the good feelings."

Our conversation then turned to her relationship with God, how she perceived him, how comfortable she felt when imagining an intimate relationship with him. I sensed Janet's frustration with finding and feeling love, and I knew that there is only one stable source in the universe. It made sense to point her in that direction.

We didn't talk anymore that day about termination. We did talk about how comfortable she felt about her psychotherapy turning into spiritual direction.

Janet's Eight Giant Leaps Home

In chapter one, Adam is assisted by a hermit, a spiritual director in making a journey back to his estranged home, Eden.

In the company of this hermit, Adam encounters three classic elements or movements of Christian formation: *willingness*—letting go of any sense of self-sufficiency; *illumination*—discovery of the monstrous inner fears that cause us to want to take matters into our hands to become self-sufficient once again; and *purgation*—burning the habitats of our deepest fears.

I believe the metaphor also suggests five additional pseudo-classic phases, or leaps. These are more subtle phases, but are often part of the process of Christian formation, and the journey of returning home. To be less metaphorical, I believe that the process of Christian formation often requires our participation in eight distinct "disciplines":

1. belief in the kingdom of God as a here-and-now reality,

2. practicing the presence of God,

3. learning to hear his voice in deep silence,

4. surrendering to the call to be willing as opposed to willful,

5. confronting our deepest fears and renouncing our most revered idols,

6. accepting our own personal crosses,

7. becoming willing to forgive, and

8. accepting and participating in reconciliation with God, and with our neighbors.

It is a process that brings us from alienation to reconciliation, from inside the cave to outside, from a distant land back to the palace in Jerusalem—a process that makes it possible to joyfully obey the two supreme commandments of Jesus, to be head-over-heels in love with God and with man.

Leaps One and Two: Being with God in His Kingdom

God must not be very flashy. After all, he created a universe in which all the really important stuff is invisible, or at least transparent. Our bodies need air, which, unless you live in Los Angeles, is unseen, and water, which, unless you live in the city where it is stored in a giant tennis shoe, has no taste. Our minds crave the intangible stimulation of thoughts and ideas; and our spirits crave the intangibles of love and relationship.[1]

When I first met Janet, her psyche was weak and withered from a lack of love. It was as emaciated as a body would be, if it were deprived of its most essential need—water. Her soul needed to be bathed in love. She needed time for its healing balm to slowly soak into each dry, parched cranny of her soul.

The solution seemed almost too easy. She needed love. God is love (1 Jn 4:8). And we are assured through Scripture, he, through the person of Jesus, will be with us always, to the very end of the age (Matt 28:20). So, at the very least, it would seem beneficial for her to learn how to (as Leanne Payne describes it) practice the presence of God, the presence of divine love.

But there were two factors working against that resolution. First, Janet was a member of a materialistic, reductionist, western society, which has little appreciation for the ephemeral. The effects of her membership were omnipresent, permeating every aspect of her life, even to the four walls of her conservative Baptist church. To practice the presence of God, Janet would have to swim against a swift current of doubt—doubt that the invisible, upside-down kingdom of Jesus really exists here and now.

As Leanne Payne observes in her book, *The Healing Presence*:

> To acknowledge the Unseen Real requires a concerted effort of the will at first. We might think of it as actually practicing the Presence. It is all too easy for us moderns to regard the supernatural world (e.g., the Holy Spirit, angels, demons) and activities (e.g., spiritual warfare) as somehow less real than the world we behold with our senses. As twentieth-century Christians, we live in a materialistic age, one in which our systems of learning have long based their conclusions on scientific truth alone. The presuppositions of such systems have misled many generations of students, blinding them to the truths of God and the Unseen Real, whether moral or spiritual.[2]

For Janet, a church-going, Bible-believing, Sunday school-teaching Christian, the concept of practicing God's presence (which is simply calling to mind the truth that God is with us) was very difficult. It was as hard for her to believe, to *really* believe, in that concept as it would have been for George Washington to fully appreciate the concept of a microwave oven. This problem was easy to solve. The story of Plato's Cave, the parables of the kingdom told by Jesus, the slow meditative readings of Leanne Payne, and readings from *The Spirit of the Disciplines*, coupled with the grace of God, slowly brought the concealed, upside-down kingdom into sharp focus for Janet.

As she began to see the unseen, it became easier for her to imagine the presence of the King. She began to do what few (other than the saints) have done. She began to will herself to be present with God. She reached over the sides of her boat and brought the dripping wet hermit on board.

But as soon as she brought the hermit aboard, another problem quickly surfaced. The hermit's presence on board with her in such close quarters made her feel very uncomfortable. Her reactions to being in his presence were very much like her reactions to being patted on the back by her boss. There was a baffling sense of fear, insecurity, and panic. If God is a coffee drinker, I'm sure he spilled it all over his lap as a result of her frantic attempts to scurry away from his touch.

However, the six months of our psychotherapy had not been wasted. Janet was no longer surprised by her reaction of fright, as she had been earlier. She now understood why she reacted to intimacy with discomfort and fear—even intimacy with God. Our work together had built roads and bridges between childhood and the present, and she was much freer to travel over them. Now she understood that she had been projecting emotions, emotions born of her father's gross mistreatment of her, onto her relationship with God. But she had also learned something profound: that insight, a matter of the head, is a necessary but insufficient requisite for change. Her insights had not descended into her heart. Despite what she *knew* about her past and about the nature of God, it was what she *felt* that was most important.

Janet needed something even more powerful than just spending time with God. She needed to be in relationship with him. And that was going to require conversation. She needed to hear from God, perhaps from across the room (if that's what felt safer to her), but she needed to hear from him.

Leap Three: Learning to Hear God

Janet began to listen to the silence. Every day she arose a half hour earlier than usual, sat in her favorite chair, and in the quietness of early morning in her home, she listened for God's voice. She strained her spiritual ears, cocked her spiritual head, and listened hard. She discovered that it was difficult to hear him at first, then it became easier, and then it became hard again.

There is a story about an old man who became weary with his wife's increasing failures to respond to his voice. He was even more frustrated by the fact that she refused to admit that she was losing her hearing. His frustration festered into anger.

One day, while she sat alone by their fire, he decided he would prove to her that she was going deaf. He called to her in a loud voice from across the room. "CAN YOU HEAR ME?" He heard no reply. He then walked in her direction, halfway across the room, and again called out, "CAN YOU HEAR ME NOW?" No reply. Then, he positioned himself just behind her back and said once again, "NOW CAN YOU HEAR ME?" She turned her head around and answered him, "Yes, honey, for the third time, YES!"

I think that this story illustrates that sometimes when we are convinced that God is going deaf, the problem may be in the ears of the hearer, and that we may have to position our own weak ears much closer to him before we discover that he has been talking the whole time.

Janet made this discovery. As she began to inch closer and closer to God in her times of silence, she found that his hearing was 20-20, and that his words were kind and comforting. The warm compassion in his words began to melt the cold fear in her heart.

After spending several weeks listening for God's voice, Janet came in for our weekly time together. She looked different. She didn't enter the room all bubbling and light-footed, as was her custom. She wasn't downcast, either. I had seen her that way on one or two rare occasions when she apparently had been unable to put on her heavy, hummingbird persona.

Instead of these extremes, she walked in, staring straight ahead as if watching some invisible movie screen, and sank into the sofa without even checking to see if it were still there. Her face showed contentment—the kind of contentment a face shows after a satisfying meal. After a few seconds of silence, she began.

Janet: God has been talking to me. I really believe that I have been hearing the voice of God.

Me: It's a rather deep voice, I suppose. (I said this with eyebrows raised to show that I wasn't serious.)

Janet: No. It's not a voice at all. It's my thoughts. I mean it's like my thoughts, anyone's thoughts, but they're not my thoughts. They're thoughts that don't belong to me, but they're playing inside my head.

Me: Well, from the look on your face, it appears that it's been a pleasant experience.

Janet: It's been a wonderful experience! I feel like I've had love letters read to me each morning for the last week.

Me: What has God been writing … saying?

Janet: That he loves me, that he has always loved me, that I am precious to him, and that he will never leave me and never forsake me, that he wants to hold me in his arms.

Me: And how are you with that? Are you comfortable hearing those letters?

Janet: Oh, yes! It feels so very real; like the God who created the entire universe is really talking, just to me. It frightens me a little. Intimacy frightens me at times and I want to run from it. But this feels pretty wonderful and ... safe. I'm very flattered. Part of me wants to crawl right up on his lap and snuggle in, and part of me wants to stay on the other side of the room. Oh, don't misunderstand me, I don't want to leave the room. I just need to get some distance between us. And it feels good ... real good."

I encouraged Janet to continue spending time with God each day, to go on listening to his voice. For several sessions we focused on her thoughts and the emotions that followed these conversations with God. At one point she made the observation that up until the time she started listening *for* God's voice, she had spent her entire prayer life talking *to* him.

I couldn't resist an analogy.

Dean Smith and Spiritual Direction

"I hear what you are saying about spending all your prayer time talking *to* God. I think that is probably true for most Christians. I know it's been true for me. Doing all the talking while 'hanging out with God,' is somewhat like being a youth league basketball coach who has won a contest that entitles him to spend an hour each day of his basketball season with Dean Smith."

Janet looked puzzled.

I continued, "The coach drives right over to the Dean's house each morning to sit and talk. But, sadly, after a number of weeks have passed and his youth league team has gone one and eight, he realizes that *he* has been doing all the talking during those sessions.

"He has told Dean about his philosophy of coaching and about all his accomplishments. He has let Dean know that he has watched almost all of the games Dean has coached. He has even pleaded for help, but he hasn't allowed Dean Smith to get a word in edgewise. Do you understand what I'm trying to say here?"

"I get it," she said, "and I wouldn't be surprised if that coach began to blame Dean Smith because his team has gone one and eight. Even though the coach never stopped talking to listen to a single word he had to say."

Janet got the point. As she continued to talk to God, the hermit was not only in the boat with her (the practice of the Presence), but they were beginning to talk. Then a problem emerged. Long before she heard the first screech of the sea monster, she had to deal with an intruder.

The Devil's Trapping Defense

Janet discovered, once again, that WGOD, with its easy-listening/inspirational format, was not the only broadcast station transmitting into the receiver of her thought-life. A loud, blaring, high-wattage station, WSIN, a station she had been listening to all her life, began to pump up its volume, apparently attempting to drown out the competition. The marketing folks at WSIN seemed to take it personally when they lost a loyal listener.

During Janet's quiet time with God, a whole host of unwanted thoughts began to play in her head. Some were simply discouraging: "This is just a lot of hocus-pocus, wishful thinking." " All these thoughts are just coming from your own head." "Wishing that God loves you doesn't make it so." "God doesn't even know your name. He's got a whole lot more important things to do than talk with you." " If he really knew you, he would turn his head and walk away."

Other intruding thoughts were graphic images. There were X-rated movies with characters from her past being projected on the screen of her mind. Within a couple of weeks of these intrusions, Janet's quiet early morning sanctuary in the corner of her living room had become perverted. She began to avoid even looking at the chair where she had sat each morning listening to love letters read by God. She quit rising early. She stopped listening for the voice of God. The dark images of sexual impurity and the loud voices of hatred and destruction caused her to run away in fear. Running away in fear felt very familiar to Janet.

Janet didn't want to talk about the dark images and thoughts that had pushed their way into her consciousness. She felt guilty that she had stopped listening to God. She felt even more guilty that such impurity was part of her inner-world. The guilt she felt caused her to slip back into old patterns of self-hatred and self-condemnation. "How could I ever believe that God would want to talk to me? How could he allow himself to be inside one whose thoughts are so immoral?"

During our sessions, I listened a lot and we talked a lot. We talked about the unconscious mind. We talked about the powerful role the past can play in the present. We talked about hummingbirds and why they stay in constant motion. And we talked about MTV.

"Janet," I said after watching her slide backwards for several weeks, "our minds are a lot like a television receiver and our thoughts are similar to the invisible television waves (I wasn't sure of the technical term, and I was hoping she didn't have cable) which are in constant motion all around us. We can't help it that MTV occupies one of the frequencies, or that its images, often lurid images, are riding around in those wave patterns. We can't stop those waves passing over and all around us."

I glanced to see if she was still tuned in. "We can't even help it if we are flipping through the channels and suddenly see and hear sexual orgies set to a demonic-cacophony of pulsating noise. You know ... MTV. However, we don't have to put down the remote, recline in our easy chair, order a pizza, and stare at the screen. We *can* help doing that. We can stop making a habit of viewing those images."

She looked deep in thought as I went on, "Conversely, there is no merit due us that we can tune in television images that unfold as great drama, literature, and art. We didn't create the programs. Even if we sent in a few bucks to the Billy Graham Crusade, we actually had little to do with a crusade occasionally being a part of our television programming. We can, however, intentionally put down the remote and become lost in what is being received. We can allow ourselves to be forever changed by what we see."

"I see what you are saying," she finally interrupted. "But, what about our own thoughts?" she asked.

"Oh," I said, trying to think fast, "that's where local-access cable comes in. We do control that."

We both smiled. But the discussion that followed let me know that she got the point I was trying to make: that she was not creating the healing voice of God, or the destructive images from Satan. She was only responsible for what she chose to watch, and for the quality of programming of her local-access channel.

I recommended to Janet that she read Peter Lord's book, *Hearing God*[3]—it had become my number one suggestion for bibliotherapy. She read it once and read it again. It became her TV guide, or perhaps it would be better to say that it became an instantaneous Siskel and Ebert review. It proved invaluable in helping her discern whether the show she watched originated in Heaven or Hollywood, or Hell.

Among the other insightful suggestions found in his book are Peter Lord's counsel that discernment, or our ability to detect whether we are hearing from God, the devil, or our own thoughts, can be facilitated by focusing on the content, relevance of content, and effects of the content of the communication.

The Content: Suppose you are married and there is a second invasion of the body snatchers and suddenly your spouse is gone. In your spouse's place is an exact replica, a look-alike, sound-alike, smell-alike reproduction. If you struck up a conversation with this imitation spouse, how would you know you were not actually talking to the person to whom you said "I do"?

Peter Lord suggests that you would know by the content of your spouse's conversation. Only the real-McCoy would know about the intimate details of the relationship, like pet-names, your secret middle name, and the fact that you thought you were supposed to take the paper anniversary seriously, and gave a copy of *The Times.*

Janet began to discover that mercy as opposed to harshness; peace-making as opposed to divisiveness; correction as opposed to condemnation; and suggestions to change yourself as opposed to insisting that another be changed, were giveaways to the fact that she was hearing from God, instead of Satan.

Relevance of Content: Janet's experience with listening for the voice of God also caused her to concur with Pastor Lord concerning the relevance of the content of the communication she heard.

If the communication she heard focused on the here-and-now, as opposed to the future; if it contained simple and practical solutions, instead of impractical-sensational ones; if it concerned the mundane matters of life, instead of the extraordinary; and if it was clear and definite, instead of complicated and confused, she felt sure that she was hearing from God. And, I believe she was right.

She liked to say, "Ya know, I believe what Mr. Lord wrote in that book. I believe God is more likely to ask me to bake my neighbor a cake than to take a boatload of Bibles to China. God knows that if he said to take the Bibles to China, I would spend the rest of my life worrying about where I'd find them and how I would get them there. I'd worry about how I would pay for the boat, and because of all my worry, I would never do anything for my neighbor."

Effects of the Content: Far and away, however, the most helpful insight concerned how the hearer felt after receiving the communication. When Janet got up from her "listening-chair" each morning filled with hope, peace, and faith, neither Peter Lord nor I had to tell her that she had heard from God. When hopelessness, worry, and fear got up from the chair with her and followed her through the day, she knew that WSIN had sent the signal that she picked up. Janet had discovered that listening to God was easy, difficult, and easy again.

It wasn't long until she felt that God told her the same thing the hermit had suggested to Adam. "Let go. You're striving much too hard. Trust me and take the oars out of the water." She did, and made an amazing discovery. She discovered the present moment.

Leap Four: Willingness

Imagine that you are sitting on the hard, wooden seat of a buckboard wagon. In your hands are thick leather reins that extend out over the sweaty backs of four horses to a metal bit each has in its mouth.

It's a beautiful day and you have decided to allow the horses to break into a rhythmic trot. You hear the steady cadence of their hooves striking a dirt path. You feel the breeze on your face as you slice slowly through the air. You look out and suddenly see that the path you are on leads straight to the gaping mouth of a Grand Canyon-sized gorge in the earth's surface.

Just as your instincts are sending a message to your frontal lobes that they will not be needed for awhile and your hands clamp down on the reins, and just nanoseconds before "PULL BACK!" sounds through your head, you hear a soft voice that whispers, "Give me the reins." You quickly turn your head and discover that you are quite alone on the wagon. You turn back toward the ravine that you are now approaching, and you hear again, "Give me the reins." You ignore the voice and pull back with all your might. The wagon slides to a stop, so close to the mouth of the gorge that you get an unwanted view of its rocky bottom. You saved your life, but in another way you also lost it.

Few would argue against the notion that the most important choice humans are faced with is the choice between willingness and willfulness—between surrender to a reality greater than oneself and self-sufficiency.

Holy Scripture presents us with a kaleidoscope of images of willing surrender: "The Lord is my shepherd ...;" "Our Father who art in heaven ... thy will be done;" "Throw down your rod, Moses;" Abraham standing over Isaac, knife drawn, willing to sacrifice his son; God's willingness to sacrifice his own Son; drops of sweat-like blood on the brow of Jesus as he says, "Nevertheless, Thy will be done;" his subsequent obedience unto death; the willingness of Paul to daily pick up his cross and follow Jesus.

Scripture is also replete with pictures of the rewards of willingness: life in the plush Garden of Eden (until the path of willfulness was chosen); green pastures and still waters; daily bread, forgiveness, and deliverance from the Evil One; the Promised Land; fatherhood of a great nation; the joy of Easter morning, and a hearty "Well done, my good and faithful servant" spoken on golden steps ascending into the kingdom.

By contrast, the Bible also gives us many pictures of what lies at the end of the path of willfulness: Satan's meteoric descent into the hell of self-sufficiency; Adam and Eve's expulsion from the garden; the murder of a brother; the dusty rubble of what had been the Tower of Babel; the wastelands of Sodom and Gomorrah; the rebuke of a lustful king; the arrogance and private hell of the Pharisees; the lifeless body of Judas swinging from a tree; and a bevy of bickering "churches" receiving letters of encouragement and correction from Paul.

As a child, Janet Weston rarely missed a Sunday school class at her small Baptist church. She was very familiar with all these images. So, it wasn't surprising when, at the age of nine, she responded to an impassioned altar call, made her way down the aisle to the front of the church, and made a sincere confession of willingness to turn her life over to Jesus. She handed him the reins.

Her encounter with the Divine produced a warm glow within her. She took it home with her, back into her cold dark home. However, the blackness in her home all but smothered the glow, reducing it to a few embers deep within her soul that refused to be put out. Janet retook the reins. Who could blame her? With a father who had been physically and sexually abusive and an emotionally abusive mother, who could fault Janet for finding ways to control her fate, slowly becoming like a slave who would work tirelessly to win compliments and approval from all the other authority figures in her life? Who could condemn her because she began to trust in her own efforts, more than the efforts of God, for her salvation? So like most Christians, she sang Sunday songs about the Great Buckboard Driver while holding tightly to the reins herself.

I would hate to be given the task of being sent to find even one Christian, living or sainted, who never retook the reins from Jesus after declaring him to be Lord of his life (I certainly couldn't pick myself). The fact that it is so commonplace for Christians to continue being their own lord while periodically meeting to sing "He is Lord," is, perhaps, the most diabolical deception of Satan.

If the very essence of the Christian life, the total surrender of our will to a compassionate Father, can pass through our fingers like water, who indeed could blame Janet for allowing willfulness to push aside willingness? Certainly not God. However, Janet's time spent practicing the presence of God and listening to his voice was not without effect. When she was strong enough to hear, these words came to her as a gentle whisper: "Let go;" "Trust me with your life;" "Become willing;" "Take your oars out of the water."

Slowly Janet began to realize that she was being called to a depth of surrender, to a level of willingness, that was far beyond what she had ever known before in her twenty-six years as a Christian. She was beginning to understand that her life had produced many barriers to true willingness, and thereby, to true Christianity.

It had taken psychotherapy, practicing the presence of God, and learning to develop a conversational relationship with him, to remove the head of her father from the shoulders of God. It took a patient God who was willing to "hang out" with her and talk to her about his love for her, to cause her father-inspired distrust to slowly erode away. And, it took God's continuous talk of her value to him to allow the level of her own

self-worth to rise to the point that an invitation to "empty herself" could produce genuine kindness to others instead of the
dry heaves.

Perhaps she described it best. "All my life, even after being
saved, I have been like a tree that has refused to let go of its
dead winter leaves. Year after year I have held on to the same
dead leaves out of fear, fear that I would have no leaves at all if
I let go of what I had. But I trusted God enough to let go and
in the letting go I have discovered springtime, with new green
leaves growing from the places where I had held onto death.
New life comes through willingness, trust, and willingness."

Slowly Janet became willing to let go of the security
afforded by doing, having, pleasing, and controlling. She let go
and discovered being. She discovered the untold wealth of the
present moment and of the marvelous mundane. She discovered that the words of the hermit were true; she had been
rowing against the current all her life. She discovered that the
miracle of willingness can cause buckboards to turn into
sleighs, and horses into reindeer.

Leap Five: Illumination of Fears and Idols

Life went very well for Janet, for a while. For weeks she
enjoyed an adventure, an odyssey available to all, in her
Father's invisible upside-down kingdom. Life became carefree
play. I once again began to think about termination of our sessions together. But before the subject was broached, the
unmistakable screech of a sea monster rang out.

Janet had a dream, a horrible nightmare, that subsequently
intruded into her waking life, slammed into her emotions and
turned her world back right-side up. It had caused her to desperately want to lunge for her "oars," to begin rowing again.

In her dream she had seen an image that to her looked like
Jesus. But his countenance was not kind, and his intent was

not pure. The image held a loosely bound bundle in its hands. It looked at Janet, its face contorted into an exaggerated sneer, and then it threw the bundle into the air.

She heard sinister laughter as the bundle spun through the air in ultra-slow motion. When it landed in her arms, she looked down into the bundle of cloth and gasped when she saw the cloth was wrapped around her own baby. She stared in frozen disbelief. The villainous image mocked her with his laughter. Then, the scene suddenly changed in a manner that is only possible in nightmares. The menacing image, which still bore the face of Jesus, was in bed with her, touching her the same sickening way her father had touched her when she was a child.

She had awakened from the nightmare in a clammy sweat; but the monstrous pictures remained painted on her conscious mind. She ran back to the safe place where she had hidden all her life before her adventure into willingness. She ran from the presence of God.

The sea monster, a projection of Janet's innermost fears, had accomplished its task. But it had also revealed something very important—Janet's deepest horror and her most powerful narcotic. Janet's nightmare and weeks of processing, exposed what she called her "number one fear." This was the last layer of the onion that needed to be peeled away.

Janet was afraid that the whole natural and supernatural world was a projection of her father. She secretly believed that nothing and no one could be trusted, not even Jesus. There were no places of safety.

She said, speaking from the deepest regions of her being: "The world will hurt me. It always has. It will use me. It will rape me and leave me crumpled and sobbing. Every square inch of it is a frightening place. There is no safe place. There is only pain."

Deep willingness had helped Janet feel some freedom for a period of time. But it helped her most by revealing that its childlike pleasures could not be fully enjoyed until her sea monster was slain.

Janet's narcotic, that which allowed her to tolerate the pain, was her ability to temporarily create good fathers who would be nurturing and kind so long as she wore a busy-as-a-hummingbird-persona, and stayed active, helpful, perfect, controlled, and servantlike.

She had learned how to turn certain teachers, pastors, and her husband, into good fathers. She wore herself out trying to earn their praise while she always stayed just on the edge of true nurture. She was always ready to dart off to a distant place of safety, always secretly afraid that they, too, were really like her own "bad father."

The hermit had climbed into Janet's boat, and she had grown increasingly comfortable in his presence. She had learned to listen to his voice. She had been obedient to his request that she let go.

And then she sat staring into the face of her deepest fear, desperately wanting to go back to her life of rowing. And all the hermit could say was: "It's not real, Janet. Let it pass through you."

Leap Six: Personal Cross

I have no doubt that God considers you to be one of his friends; he would not trust you with so many crosses, sufferings, and humiliations. Crosses are God's means of drawing souls closer to himself. And these crosses accomplish his purposes much more rapidly and effectively than all our personal efforts put together. Crosses destroy self-love at its very root, down in the depths of the human spirit where we can hardly detect it. But God knows where it is lodged, and he attacks it in its greatest strongholds.

Fenelon
Let Go

During the past two decades there has been a resurgence of interest in spirituality. This has been reflected in the creation of a multitude of seminars, journal articles, and books on spirituality by Christians and non-Christians, pastors and psychologists.

As a professor in a graduate program which attempts to integrate psychological truth with Christian faith, I have read and discussed much of this new material with great interest, and I have developed a brief litmus test for heresy. I look for two crosses—the cross of Jesus, and a personal cross of each individual. If both are not present in the new teachings I hear about, I don't want to become a new learner of them.

Janet's journey back home involved both crosses. She was well aware that it was the cross that opened the gates to his kingdom; and that it was his cross, victory over death, and ascent into heaven that caused the hermit (the Holy Spirit) to be present with her. And she soon encountered her own personal cross.

Janet became aware that she must make herself face her deepest fear without the benefit of a non-prescription pain killer. She gradually began to sense that she was being called to flush away her ability to manufacture and control good fathers. Fortunately, she was provided an awake-dream that helped her understand and accept this cross. In spite of the horrible image of Jesus that had been imposed on Janet's mind, she continued to rise early and spend time listening to God. One morning a powerful vision played in her inner theater.

In this vision she saw herself standing in the middle of a great room which appeared to be a museum. The floor was polished marble. The ceiling was polished marble. The columns that held up the ceiling were polished marble. There were no windows in the room, but it was softly aglow from the light of a large chandelier and the reflection of that light by a thousand-and-one spots of reflective brightness on the marble floor, ceiling, and columns.

The room was sparsely decorated by oil paintings and sculptures. Janet described her role in the museum as combination curator and maid. Occasionally someone would enter the museum and she would show him around. She felt a great sense of pride in each piece of art. She noticed that she was greatly distressed by any dirt or grime tracked in by the visitors. As soon as they left, and sometimes before they left, she would busy herself getting rid of the dirt and putting the shine back on the marble.

At some point in this awake-dream Janet felt compelled to walk toward the back of the large room. Arriving at the large back wall of marble, she was surprised to find two old weathered, wooden doors. The doors looked like they should have been attached to a barn and were kept from opening into the museum by a roughly-hewn crossbeam. The beam was supported by four wrought-iron supports—two to a door.

At that point in her vision, Janet felt that she was being asked, by some unseen presence, to lift the beam and let the doors swing open. She didn't want to obey this urging. In fact she could think of nothing she would rather do less than open those doors. But with much angst and trepidation she lifted the heavy wooden brace and allowed the doors to slowly swing open.

In the vision she gasped in horror. Sitting in her chair in her living room she gasped in horror. The doors were pushed open by a slow-moving mass of liquid sludge, murk, mire, and assorted garbage. The dirty black and brown filth oozed in and over her shoes and across the polished marble floors of her museum. It belched in from the opening with a stench that would cause a maggot to turn its head in disgust.

Janet stared out of the now wide-open doors in horror. There was nothing but sludge in view as far as she could see. Her impulse, and it was a locomotive-sized impulse, was to push the doors closed and to brace them again with the wooden beam.

Her heels were already lifted from the ground as her body started to give in to that impulse. But she again heard the voice. It said, "Stay where you are. Leave the doors open."

"But I've got to clean this up!" she cried.

"No," came the reply. "I'll clean it up."

She resisted the urge to close the doors. She resisted the urge to run for a mop. She stood her ground in the midst of the sludge, which was now knee deep. She stood her ground and in doing so, bore her cross.

Just at the point where she felt that she could take it no more, she was aware of a touch on her shoulder. She turned and looked into the face of Jesus. She heard, "Yes, this time it's really me. I'll stand here with you." She felt a warm peace, and then she heard, "Look through the doors."

She looked through the opening and above descending murk and mire she saw, far off in the distance, beams of sunlight. She saw birds flying. She saw the tops of mountains. She continued to stare into the distance for a long period of time as a gorgeous painting slowly unfurled before her eyes. She was so captivated by the beauty of the outside world that she did not even notice as the last of the black, grimy sludge was pushed past her feet and out the front of the museum by clear, sparkling water.

When she finally felt the cold, pristine water on her feet, she turned in amazement to see that the room was clean again. She had done nothing to make it so. And it was bathed by sunlight streaming in through the open back and front doors. She looked into the face of a beaming Jesus, who said something to this effect, "I do windows, too."

The retelling of her vision had deeply moved Janet. It was obvious that it had afforded her a profound insight. I wasn't about to mess that up with my own analysis. So I simply said, "What does the vision mean to you?"

"I think it means that I have spent my entire life scurrying around to be worthy of praise and recognition from others. It means that I have kept a dark, murky secret bolted away in my subconscious mind. But in keeping those doors locked, I have also locked out creativity, spontaneity, intuition, and a part of me that can have more open access to God and his kingdom."

"And what do you make of the role of Jesus in the vision?" I asked.

"Oh, I think he wanted to show me that the other picture—you know, from the other dream—was not him. I think he wanted me to know that there is a lot of pain attached to 'letting go,' but that he is there, right by my side, helping me to get through it. I think I must have felt what a drug addict feels when he quits taking a drug—withdrawal. I mean, while I was standing there in the midst of all that crap, I wanted so desperately to make my room clean and acceptable again. Just allowing that dream to continue was the hardest thing I've ever done. I had the shakes. I mean in real life, just watching it, I had the delirium tremors."

As her counselor, I was glad that I was finally learning when to keep my mouth shut. I knew that I didn't even deserve an assist on that one. God had slammed home the winning basket all by himself.

In the following weeks, strengthened by her vision, Janet was able to face her own personal cross—the pain of facing life without allowing herself to earn the praise of good fathers (cleaning her museum); and the pain of allowing the doors to her subconscious to remain open. In through those open doors blew the winds of Easter morning.

But there was one final obstacle to deal with first—the flames of purgation.

Leap Seven: The Pain of Forgiveness

If I go to the library at the university where I teach and do a CD-ROM search on "assertiveness," I will find hundreds and hundreds of references to published articles and books.

If I change the descriptor and look for published material on forgiveness I will find precious few references (and the majority, less than ten, will be for articles found in "religious" journals).

If I give the first list to one of our librarians, she can help me redeem the printout of references for hundreds of articles and scores of books that will help me learn how to teach my clients to say: "Excuse me, but I ordered this hamburger well-done and it looks like it needs a tourniquet!" I could not possibly read all the material on assertiveness our library contains in a year's time, even with the benefit of an Evelyn Wood speed reading course. However, I could read all of the journal articles on forgiveness, material that could help me and my clients saw through the ropes that bind us to the past—without feeling any hunger pains, or having to worry about eye strain. Something is wrong.

I hadn't been in a clinical practice long until I realized I had a far greater need for the forgiveness articles than for the ones on assertiveness. I rarely worked with a client where there was not an obvious need to help him facilitate forgiveness. I was embarrassed by my lack of knowledge about forgiveness. I was embarrassed by my lack of experience with this intervention. But I was also red-faced embarrassed at the thought of ever having to justify forgiveness as the treatment of choice to some insurance company. So I generally tried everything else first.

With Janet, however, as with most clients, the road to health eventually led to forgiveness. My resources were very limited. They included: a book, *Forgive and Forget*, written by an ethics professor, Lewis Smedes; a scene from the movie *The Mission*; and a two-by-four analogy I heard in a class taught by Archibald Hart. I would need all three for Janet.

Janet had come a long way since our time spent correcting maladaptive behaviors and thoughts. She had learned to practice the presence of the Great Physician and to hear his voice; and she had learned that deep, dark images of her father could pervert those special experiences of God. She had learned and experienced new depths to the surrender of her will. She had played in God's kingdom, and she had stared down a sea monster. And with the help of the hermit, she had faced her life without her most cherished narcotic.

There was, however, one final problem. Janet had not truly and totally forgiven her father for the perverted atrocities he had subjected her to. She had not forgiven him for stealing her childhood and her innocence. She had not forgiven him for filling her thoughts with self-reproach and her dreams with darkness. And she did not want to forgive him. She held on to her anger with white knuckles.

Scenes from a Movie

In the movie, *The Mission*, one of the characters, a slave trader named Mendoza, discovers that his girlfriend has fallen in love with his cherished brother while Mendoza was away in the jungles of South America capturing, murdering, and selling human beings.

In a tragic scene that follows, Mendoza kills his brother with a knife. He then goes to live in a small cell at a Jesuit mission and waits to die a slow death of remorse and starvation. He declares, "For me, there is no redemption. There is no penance enough for me."

A priest, played by Jeremy Irons, takes on the liberation of Mendoza as a mission. He proposes a harsh penance to which Mendoza agrees.

Mendoza agrees to go into the jungle with several priests to help them build a mission. He agrees to go while dragging what must surely be two hundred pounds of weaponry, bound together by rope mesh. Eventually, after several episodes in which he is nearly pulled to his death by the weight of the weapons, he arrives at the village where the natives live, the very same community he has ravaged in the past. Although he has arrived at the destination, the pain drawn by mud-caked lines on his face show that the penance has not been effective.

Then, a young man, a native, pulls out a knife and walks toward Mendoza. The audience is unsure how the knife will be used. Mendoza seems sure. His face grimaces, but his eyes seem to be welcoming a life-stealing slice of his throat. The native then looks past his neck, bends down, and begins to saw through the thick rope that has kept Mendoza a prisoner of his weapons. He separates Mendoza from his burden, and then rolls the weapons over a ledge and into the river. He gives Mendoza his life back, twice.

Then, in what is one of the most powerful scenes I have ever witnessed, Mendoza washes his cheeks with tears of release, tears of joy. He is forgiven by someone who has the right to take his life. In this act he is finally released.

I used that image as a picture of how Janet needed to find and allow forgiveness as a wonderfully "selfish" act. That is, apart from biblical and theological reasons to forgive, Janet needed to forgive because the weight of her anger would surely pull her to the jagged rocks below. It would bar her entrance to Eden.

While embarrassed that her motivation to forgive was not pure, Janet, nonetheless, became willing to begin the process. She said at one point, "I can't believe I want to hold on to this hot coal. It's burning my skin. But God help me, I want to keep holding on to it."

Two-by-Fours and Forgiveness

In a lecture by Arch Hart on anger, he used an analogy to describe how most of what is taught about forgiveness is not about forgiveness. Rather it is about two extremes, premature forgiveness, and post-mature forgiveness.

"Imagine," he said, "that you are standing over a person who has done you great harm. He is sitting in a chair in front of you. He is tied and cannot move."

"You have a two-by-four in your hand. You raise it over your head to strike the one who has given you pain. But before you bring it down on him, you decide that you must forgive him. You throw the plank away. You say, 'I forgive you. I must.' And you walk away. But this is not forgiveness. It is premature forgiveness. Your anger still burns within."

"Imagine next that you are standing over the person, you have a two-by-four poised to strike. Your anger says, 'Pay him back ... an eye for an eye.'

"And you say, 'Good idea,' and beat him with the board. This feels good. Catharsis feels good. But, of course, this is not forgiveness. It is post-mature forgiveness. It is retaliation."

He went on to explain that true forgiveness falls somewhere

between the two extremes. It involves picking up the two-by-four and raising it over your head. It involves recounting the pain you experienced, feeling it again, and knowing that you have the "right" to hurt him for what he has done.

True forgiveness is not denial or repression. But it is not retaliation either. With true forgiveness you must throw down the plank. Perhaps it will take Jesus' entering the picture to pry it from your hands, but you must throw it down. You must cry. You must hurt. And you must hug him and walk away.

Dr. Hart said no more about forgiveness, but I never once thought about asking for my money back. In fact, that one analogy was worth the price of the course. That is because I heard him say that true forgiveness is an act of grace. All we can do as psychotherapists is to facilitate that act by helping ensure that clients do not settle for pre- or post-mature forgiveness.

The analogy helped Janet to realize that all of her previous attempts to forgive her father had been premature, and it helped her to own up to the fact that her present desire was to beat a dead man senseless.

Forgive and Forget

It was the book, *Forgive and Forget*,[4] by Lewis Smedes that helped Janet understand more about the middle-ground of forgiveness—true forgiveness. As she read that wonderful book she realized that the hurt, the anger, and the hatred she felt actually could be stages of forgiveness; that forgiveness is a process that takes time; that the process is not easy; and that to make it work, she must learn to see her father and herself in a new light. As she did these things, she met God and he did the rest. Slowly an iceberg of hatred for her father melted and ran into an ocean of forgiveness. She never forgot the past. But it became irrelevant.

Leap Eight: Reconciliation

Shortly before Janet and I finally terminated, she told me of one more wide-awake dream. In her dream she saw herself in a dark room. She was very frightened. In her hand was a sword. She began to swing it at the darkness. A kind voice said, "Put down the sword and come over here."

She obeyed the voice, letting the sword clunk to the floor. Still afraid of the darkness and its possible contents, she made her way across the room in the direction of the voice.

"Yes," the voice said, "you are here. Crawl up on my lap." The voice was so soothing that she did not fear. She climbed up onto a warm lap. "Now," said the voice, "turn on the light."

She felt her way across the face of a wall until she felt a light switch. She turned it on and the room was filled with a warm glow. Now she could see. The voice and the lap belonged to Jesus. She nestled into his embrace. He spoke again, "This is the best way to fight the darkness, not with swords and armor, but by climbing into my lap and turning on the light."

When Janet told me about this vision, I knew that she had made the trip all the way back home. I could almost smell the fish frying on the fire. I could almost see the hermit transformed into a dove. I did see Janet's smiling face. I did see a hummingbird at rest on the lap of her best Friend—in the throne room of her heart.

7

Reconciliation:
This Time It's Personal

We shall not cease from exploration
And the end of all our exploring
Will be to arrive where we began
And know the place for the first time.

T.S. Eliot

"Father Gibbon has decided to put you in the bishop's room," she said while pushing open the heavy glass door at the entrance to Holy Family Retreat House.

From the look on her face, the expression of one offering an expensive gift, I knew I must be in for a serious upgrade from the Spartan conditions I had always encountered as a semi-regular visitor.

I followed her across the lobby, that was strewn with sleeping bags, towels, junk food, and teddy bears belonging to the members of the Colonial High School Drum and Fife Corps, up a stairwell marked "private," and down a long narrow hall-way, deep into the bowels of the priests' quarters. I felt very privileged, and a little holier than usual.

She stopped outside of the "Bishop's Suite," located the key in a deep pocket, and unlocked the maple-stained door. It swung open on well-oiled hinges and revealed the contents of the room. I pushed my jaws back together and tried not to show my dismay.

I had expected that the title "bishop" would command, at minimum, a three-room suite with plush carpet, gold-plated whatnots, and a sunken baptistery with hot and cold holy-water.

What I saw was a ten foot by twelve foot cubicle with institutional-green, cinder-block walls and Salvation-Army amenities. The only discernible upgrades from the other sixty Spartan rooms were a brown, cracked-vinyl easy chair, a slightly over-sized desk, and glass (instead of stamped-metal) ash trays. This wasn't an upgrade. I didn't even smoke.

As I entered the room, I couldn't help the feeling that I was passing through a time-warp to arrive back at youth camp. It was only the easy chair and a wooden crucifix over the desk that assured me I had not. (It is very rare to find crucifixes in Protestant youth camps.) I smiled and thanked her profusely.

I had decided, just the day before, at the insistence of my wife, to check myself and my computer into a retreat house until I had finished this book. The reasoning was that until it was completed, I was not fit for human interaction anyway.

It had been almost ten years since the rowing analogy had percolated up into my conscious mind. I could still vividly remember the occasion. I had been driving through the rural countryside of southeastern Wisconsin when it surprised me. It had been almost five years since the images of that allegory had become bright lime-green words on the black face of my computer screen. And now, as my family and I were preparing to pack up our belongings and travel back to our beloved rural Georgia (after five long years in the city), it seemed time to peck out "the end" on the last page of this project, put it in a box, and tape it down. So, not knowing if I would be in the Bishop's Suite for two hours or two weeks, I began to conclude.

Does It Play in Peoria?

In this book I have proposed that there is a deep homesickness within the human heart which has endured for millennia. The homesickness is a longing for Eden, a longing to return to a simpler time when we lived in love instead of fear—to the last time that life made perfect sense.

I have proposed that the unavoidable compassion deficits we experience in life, as a normal part of development, cause deep pains that can either turn us more fervently toward the heaven of our true home, or toward the hell of self-sufficiency. We attempt self-sufficiency as a pain management strategy to the extent that we use the behavioral narcotics of power and control to deaden the pain. We attempt self-sufficiency when we listen to the voice of our false self.

But the voice of the true self can also be heard. It is the voice that suggests we should cure our homesickness by allowing our true self to come back home. It suggests that we drop the needle, spill the pills, tape shut the mouth of the false self, and plop back down on the throne.

I have proposed that there are at least eight classic movements which are part of our homeward-bound journey:

- believing in the outside-the-cave-world of the kingdom of God,
- practicing the presence of God,
- learning to discern his voice,
- embracing willingness,
- overcoming the fears and idols which cause us to desire willfulness once again,
- crawling up on our own personal cross,
- forgiveness,
- reconciliation.

While I have presented a progression of case studies that have provided snapshots from the travelogues of several clients, I have avoided something painful. I haven't written about the journey of my own life. I haven't told you how it played in Peoria.

Compassion Deficits

If I were ever invited to give my testimony at a breakfast meeting of Promise Keepers or the Full Gospel Business Men's Fellowship, it wouldn't be long before most of the audience would be sleeping in their eggs. If I gave my testimony on the "700 Club," it would be a ratings nightmare. And I am sure it will be decades before Geraldo gets around to doing a show on white, Anglo-Saxon, Protestant males who have lived relatively bland lives—at least bland relative to the lives of one-armed chain saw jugglers who drink heavily.

My sins, though they be many, have been of the mundane variety. I have neither abused nor been abused. I've never even started a chain saw. And to make matters worse, there has never been one minute in my life that I have felt unloved by my parents. I came close to feeling that way for a full minute once when I was ten.

My father is a very saintly man and a retired minister. He somehow managed to stay far away from church politics while serving his denomination for over fifty years. Once, during the time when formal operations thinking was pushing aside concrete operations in my ten-year-old brain, I was troubled by the thought that perhaps my father was more devoted to his own holiness than to me. I set a trap for him.

While sitting around the supper table one evening I asked him, "What would you do if someone broke into our house, with a gun in his hand, and asked if I were in the house?" In the scenario I had carefully constructed for my father, he knew that I was hiding in my room. I wanted to see if he loved me enough to lie.

When my father didn't give an immediate answer, I blurted out, "You mean you wouldn't lie, even to save my life?" He said nothing. And for just to the west of a minute, I felt unloved. During that time I believe I even shouted something like, "So, you love the church more than me!" I remember that he looked very solemn, and more than a little hurt.

He said, "I wouldn't lie to him, and I wouldn't tell him where you were either." For a moment I was puzzled; then my mother put my thoughts into words. "He would die before he would let anyone hurt you; and he would die before he would lie."

I felt very ashamed. Those few seconds were the only time in my life I ever wondered whether or not I was loved. When they had passed, I knew these two, my parents, would lay down their lives to save me. So what could I possibly know about compassion deficits? Plenty!

Smiley Blanton, co-founder with Norman Vincent Peale of The American Foundation of Religion and Psychiatry, wrote a wonderful book titled, *Love or Perish.*[1]

The book focuses on the universal need for love and the subsequent battles between love and love's enemies, fear and hatred, in the development of the person.

After making the case that fear and hatred accelerate our journey toward death while love promotes life, the author comforts overly perfectionist parents by assuring them that compassion deficits are inevitable—no matter how much love is felt for a child.

There will be unavoidable gaps of time between the time an infant feels hunger pains and when he gets fed. During those gaps the child will fear that neither food nor parent is forthcoming and become pretty angry about the situation. The child will experience compassion deficits and subsequent fear and anger, even if the parent has ears the size of an elephant and wears track shoes to bed. Additionally, parents cannot always *be* present. They will inevitably be called away, whether it is to earn money to pay for all the Pampers, or to tend to boiling oatmeal.

My father was always pastor of small, country churches that could not support our family. He always worked a second job. Even two jobs didn't provide enough to keep us housed, clothed, and fed. So my mother also worked as a school teacher.

I loved my parents, and I knew they loved me. But during the time that their love was not physically present, I experienced compassion deficits. While I was never hit, kicked, abused, or burned with a cigarette, love could not always be present. Its absence hurt like the devil.

Behavioral Narcotics

Cousin Rodney was my best friend growing up. We usually spent the entire summer together, turning our yards into golf courses by burying empty bean cans in the dirt, perfecting the art of chipping golf balls over houses using only a putter, playing games of "500" (baseball for two), and running through the woods shooting at each other with sticks.

One day, when we were in my room recuperating from all the calorie-burning out in the sticky, Georgia heat, Rodney started walking toward a converted book shelf in my room. The shelf held a collection of my favorite toys. Just as Rodney was lifting a plastic airplane from its stand for a closer inspection and perhaps a test flight across the room, I heard myself exclaim, "No, not those toys. They're just for display."

Rodney drew back his head so far that it was no longer centered over his body. I'll never forget the puzzled look on his face. And it wasn't because his eight-year-old cousin had correctly used the word display. It was at the very idea of toys being used for anything else but play. His facial expression was confirmation of something I had suspected. Neatly arranging toys for exhibition is a little weird, especially for an eight year old. But Rodney was a good friend. He never let on to the Johnson boys.

Fifteen years later I was sitting outside the office of the man who would be my advisor and mentor during the time I would spend pursuing graduate degrees in psychology and theology. I had never met him, never laid eyes on him. I sat in an outer office and tried to construct a picture of him by listening to his voice as he spoke with a colleague by telephone. I did know his reputation. It was the stuff academic legends are made of. I was very excited.

He hung up the phone. The sound of pen on paper came through the open door; then he invited me into his office. I sat down, and before my head could stop my heart, it told my mouth to ask a question. "How long do you plan to be at Fuller?"

He didn't look puzzled like cousin Rodney. He simply answered my question. "I plan to retire here," and he then followed with questions of his own. I knew that I had just engaged in another weirdism. There had been quite a string of them in the time between the interaction with cousin Rodney and this one with my advisor. There was no doubt about it. Over the course of my life I had become addicted to several different "behavioral narcotics." I had become a perfectionist—wanting all things in my environment neat and in order. And, as my initial conversation with my advisor indicated, I wanted all things valuable to me controlled, stable, and stationary.

During my experiences with compassion deficits a phenomenon occurred which Smiley Blanton discusses in *Love or Perish.* He suggests that when love is distant we become easy prey to the dread emotions of fear and resentment, anxiety and guilt. These are the emotions which are cast out by perfect love, but which rush in to quickly fill the void left when love is absent. I suspect the devil keeps them in a pressurized container, just waiting for an opportunity to pump them into our psyches.

To make a long story short, I quickly learned to depend on behavioral narcotics to minimize pain caused by my fears—fears of abandonment and fears of insignificance. I became a card-carrying perfectionist. I set ridiculously high standards for myself and those around me. And I became over-controlling of valuable objects—especially the people whose love I needed most. Perfectionism, over-achievement, and control have been good "highs" for me. But, more often than not, they have also left me in the gutter.

True and False Self

Philip St. Romain, in his book, *Becoming a New Person: Twelve Steps to Christian Growth*,[2] proposes that there is a motive for almost all human behavior. He suggests that three of the most common motives are:

- pleasure—gratification of sensual needs,
- esteem—our need to be regarded favorably by others, and
- security—our desire to minimize the likelihood that misfortune, sickness, or death will overtake us prematurely.

At first reading I was tempted to minimize this synthesis of human motivations. But then I recalled the respective (albeit exclusive) claims of Sigmund Freud, Friedrich Nietzsche, and Erich Fromm that the basic human urges are for pleasure

(Freud), for power (Nietzsche), and for security as a means to escape loneliness (Fromm).

I then recalled the wilderness-temptation of Jesus as presented in Luke 4:1-15 (my paraphrase of NIV) when Satan attempted to derail Jesus' life and ministry by appealing to his desire for pleasure: "If you are God's Son, command this stone to turn into a loaf of bread." His desire for esteem or power: "To you I am ready to give the whole extent of this vast empire and its splendor. It has been put at my disposal, and I give it to whom I please." And to his desire for security: "If you are God's Son, fling yourself down from this place. The Scripture says: 'To his angels he will give charge of you to keep you safe.'" Through it all, however, Jesus prevailed over his human urges, resisted the devil and his vials of narcotics. The rest is Easter!

I even pondered how these basic motivations, which Romain proposes, may be seen as arising out of our tripartite nature of body (pleasure), mind (esteem, power), and spirit (security, relationship). But at that point I was beginning to feel that I had left the electric-milking machine on the cow long after she was dry.

Ah, but what does this hemorrhaging of synthesis have to do with the true and false self, or with airplanes and mentors? The pain of compassion deficits may serve to intensify these basic human motivations, in a similar fashion to how forty days of fasting can make rocks look pretty tasty.

The true and false selves offer very different solutions. The false self, echoing the voice of Satan, urges us to allay the pain caused by compassion deficits through the pleasure of gratification, the glory of narcissistic accomplishments, and the security of being able to control those we need. These narcotics are very hard to resist when our psyches are suffering from love anemia.

The true self knows that these solutions are short-sighted

and ultimately deadly. It suggests that our desire for pleasure can only be fulfilled by the joy of abundant life in God's kingdom; our desire for esteem can only be fulfilled by recognizing that the Maker of trees and butterflies is also our loving Daddy who died for us; our desire for security and relationship can only be satisfied through realizing that we are, in fact, immortal spiritual beings who get to live forever in community.

These are high-sounding words. The fact is, until very recently, I listened only to the suggestions of my false self and attempted to find pleasure, esteem, and security through perfectionism, manipulation, and control. Day after day, I flunked the desert test, circling the wilderness, instead of crashing Canaan.

Eight Leaps Back Home
The Kingdom of God

I was sitting in a Sunday school room for five year olds when I first started believing in the kingdom of God as a potential residence. Of course, as I mentioned in chapter one, I was a full-grown seminary student at the time. From the time the film projector sputtered to a stop, after the showing of Plato's Cave, until this present moment, ten years and a few thousand movies later, things have never been the same.

I slowly came to believe that there really is a "kingdom." Life in the kingdom is as different from life in the world as substance is from shadow. The kingdom's value structure is upside down and inside out to that of Madison Avenue. Fairy tales become cherished because they remind the child in us that if we can muster enough childlike faith, it's possible to live in the kingdom. Jesus came to earth to invite his "lost sheep" to come back to the pastures of the kingdom. It is also why he was put to death. This kingdom is a here and hereafter reality.

I also came to believe that to live there, we must be willing to die to here. And that navigating the trip to Bountiful, a trip that begins in our own heart and ends in his, depends about ninety-nine percent on grace and divine energy, and about one percent on works and human willingness.

But by withholding our one percent, we can turn a child's game of leapfrog into a lifetime of circling in the wilderness. We must be willing to make the Eight Leaps—the second one being the moment-by-moment practice of God's presence.

Practice of the Presence

I was always pretty good in math. Somehow, even through advanced algebra and trigonometry, it just made sense. One minus one equals zero. What else could it equal? Zero plus one equals one again. Yep. I can follow that. It also seemed to follow that if a person minus love equals zero, then it is love that needs to be added back. I knew from Sunday school, that God equals love (1 Jn 4:7). Therefore, the cure for compassion deficit is to practice the presence of a loving God. It's elementary.

But that's where it stopped being simple. The idea of practicing the presence of God, having him with me twenty-four hours a day, in the car, office, bed, bathroom, was a bit unsettling. Being known is scary. Being known by the Divine, the One who told Moses to take his shoes off because his presence made the ground holy, and who would not allow Moses the privilege of eye contact, is terrifying.

T.E. Lawrence, in *Seven Pillars of Wisdom*, tells about traveling in the Arab world and being told of a crazy man who was singing about the love of God. When he asked how his informer knew the man was crazy, the reply came, "Because he was singing about the love of God."[3] The implication is that the idea of a personal loving God is ... well ... away from the norm. Indeed, even in Scripture the notion does not reach full crescendo until God becomes embodied in the man, Jesus.

Even as a complete novice to the idea of practicing the presence of God, I could immediately see several obstacles one might have to hurdle in trying to practice his presence. I believe that at least four of these are: bad theology, bad psychology, good drugs, and bad *heilsgeschichte*.

Bad *heilsgeschichte*.

This is one of the few German words that stuck with me from my time in seminary. (The others are *Weiner schnitzel* and *brauchwurst*). *Heilsgeschichte* refers to salvation history—the progressive story of a plan for salvation that germinates in Genesis and matures throughout the following sixty-five books. Knowing that the story of salvation is dynamic and progressive means that it is not crazy for God to reveal himself as terrifying in some passages of Genesis and as the compassionate Christ of the Gospels or the *Abba* (Daddy) to the apostle Paul.

In a similar fashion, my children may have memories of me as a towering giant who smacked them on the hand when they were two years old and were headed for the electrical outlet with a hairpin in hand and, as a loving daddy who holds them in his lap and wipes away their tears when a friend has been unkind. Some day they will know that both memories expressed my love. I think they already do.

My point is that those who have images of God only as the towering giant of the Old Testament will be less excited about practicing his presence, until new images of him as Brother, Friend, and Daddy can be found.

Bad theology.

The comedian Kurt Cloninger produced a video tape in which he acts out six common misconceptions about the nature of God that result from the exaggeration of one truth about God at the expense of all other truths. Since the exaggeration of a truth at the expense of THE TRUTH is heresy, he is acting out six common, heretical ways we view God.

In the skits he gives a comic performance of God as a cosmic sheriff out to catch transgressors, a hyperactive shop foreman concerned only with productivity, a senile grandfather with a failing memory, a polite waiter anxious to take our "orders," a party animal who just wants us to feel good, and a ninety-eight-pound weakling who has been placed in a box by the members of a church. It is a very creative portrayal of six, all-too-common, heretical views of God. Here we have six "gods" whose presence no one would want to practice, except a sadist or narcissist. Cloninger concludes by offering his "view" of God, the Father, waiting the return of his prodigal son with arms outstretched and a heart full of compassion. It is only this seventh God-view which gives us a picture of the God by whose side we would want to stand.

Bad theology.

I have observed in my almost-a-decade of clinical practice that clients invariably create images of God in which they place the head of one of their parents on divine shoulders. In doing so, they not only create heresy, they create a God whose presence they do not wish to practice.

Good drugs.

Many people become satisfied with the temporary and fading relief provided by the use of their behavioral narcotic of choice— their strategies devised to ease the pain from compassion deficits. These people avoid practicing God's presence for the same reasons a heroin addict might prefer not to "shoot up" with his mother in the room.

I am guilty of all of the above. I have not allowed my childish perceptions of God as a strict parent to mature into the vision of a God who wants to call me "friend." I have viewed God as a cosmic sheriff and shop foreman. In so doing, I have sought to avoid being in the same room where six-shooters (the props of a cosmic sheriff) or time clocks (the props of a shop foreman) might be present. At times I have also recreated God in the image of my parents, and I have wanted to avoid him so that he would not see me as I kept my fears at bay through the use of perfectionism and control. But slowly and surely he has begun to bathe my brain with different images—images of a Father who travels again and again down a long dusty path to spend the day waiting by the highway for his prodigal son's return. I have the image of a Father who gets lost in the pleasure of playing with his toddling child, the image of a Friend who emptied himself of his divinity so that we could talk together, man-to-man, the image of a Daddy who tucks me in at night and reads me the children's story *Love You Forever*.[4]

With these pictures and because of his patience, I have slowly become comfortable spending more and more time practicing the presence of Love. I have learned to "bear the beams of love," as William Blake puts it, for several minutes each day. And sometimes, when I'm on retreat, I can bear them for close to an hour.

Listening to Love

My time in clinical practice has taught me at least one thing. Robert Lewis Stevenson once said, "People, all people, sit on the threshold of their personalities and call out to the world for someone who will come and love them." Wouldn't it be great if Someone, some omnipotent and omniscient Someone, would stop by for a chat?

Ari L. Goldman in his book, *The Search for God at Harvard*, makes the following observation. "Theology is, simply put, the study of God and of God's relationship to the universe. The word comes from the Greek words *theo*, meaning 'God,' and *logos*, meaning 'discourse.'"[5] Theology is "God-talk"—discourses about God and by God.

Goldman points out that God-talk is more of a Christian concern than a Jewish one, and suggests that "religion," from the Latin *religare*, meaning "to bind back" (to the past), somehow seems more Jewish.

Concerning theology—God talk—there are many who believe God is a veritable chatterbox (see Peter Lord's book, *Hearing God*). One who is willing to dialogue with his children twenty-four hours a day retelling his own theology, personalizing the love, but changing nothing else. Indeed, John in his Gospel tells us that it is by being able to know God's voice that we can follow him instead of a stranger (Jn 10:1-6).

An always-present, loving God who dialogues with us is very good news. But learning to discern God's voice and separate it from that of the stranger (Satan), and from our own internal dialogue, takes practice. But practice we must, if we are ever going to recognize the voice of the gentle Shepherd, the only one who can lead us back home.

In early January of 1974 in a college class, I sat next to Steve, my best friend from high school. We were waiting for biology class to begin. It was our second quarter in college, and we were both still a little nervous about being able to capture all the fast-flowing information. But before the professor even opened his mouth to offer his first pontification, I got a lesson in biology. A beautiful college freshman with flowing brown hair, green eyes, and an armload of books entered the room and headed in our direction. My hormones immediately held an impromptu rodeo.

I leaned over and with a flushed face whispered to Steve, "I'm going to marry her." I don't think she heard me, because she didn't seem frightened. She walked between us, and she sat down right behind me. I don't think she heard a thousand little hormones hollering "Yee-ha!"

I was seventeen years old. My dating experience had been somewhat limited by the fact that my growth spurt didn't arrive until I was in the eleventh grade, but I had never made such an immature statement before, and I was not given to bouts of discernment. But time proved that I had spoken prophetically. In less than three years that beautiful young woman and I were married.

My relationship with Regina in many ways parallels my relationship with God. Regina (I call her Jeanie) took away my breath. She also took away my appetite. For the next few days after I first saw her, my stomach lost its single-minded attraction toward all things edible. My appetite eventually came back, but for more than a year I would lose it again every time she would return to campus after an absence of a few days or more. I got so skinny I had to put rocks in my pocket on windy days to keep me from being blown away.

With all the racing hormones, fluctuating appetite, and uncontrollable prophetic utterances, I knew I must be in love. (Fortunately I hadn't studied about manic episodes yet.) But I played it cool. I had seen a few James Bond movies and I didn't want to appear too eager. I waited until I could keep a cheeseburger down—almost a week—before I told her. She seemed genuinely flattered, but didn't do the humane thing and reciprocate in kind. She didn't say anything about how she felt about me. I barely made it home before I lost the cheeseburger.

After a while, I found some composure somewhere, and we settled into a wonderful dating relationship. After a few months, Jeanie told me there was something she wanted to say.

It was a Saturday afternoon. We walked inside a classroom building and sat on the steps. There was no one else around. I sat and waited. My heart was making the buttons on my shirt move to its rhythm. I waited. But her lips were not moving.

I stared at her mouth, hoping to see the words forming before they came out. Nothing. A period of time, something like the time needed to fight the Hundred Years War passed. And then I heard it: "I love you." Suddenly life made sense! My hormones were throwing confetti! With time, my biology settled down, and we passed on through that initial phase of infatuation and into the less exciting, but more rewarding, phases of perspiration, and maturation, and commitment, and consummation.

The experience of being in Jeanie's presence and listening to her voice has in many ways paralleled my relationship with God. In both relationships there have been initial periods of infatuation with cascading feelings of joy and well-being; the rehearsal of future conversations because I didn't want to run out of something to say; the desire to be truly known and intense fears about the possibility of being truly known; self-protective game playing; and last the harmful effects of "bad theology" and "bad psychology."

There are other parallels, resemblances concerning communication. In both relationships there have been times of being together in which I have talked and not listened; listened and not talked; refused to listen because of anger; refused to talk because of anger; felt truly heard and deeply understood; and experienced communication beyond and without words.

And, during special times of contemplation before God, I have sat in his presence with no one else around. I have looked into his face and stared at his lips, attempting to get a glimpse of his words before they are spoken. And after waiting for periods of time which have been just this side of eternity, I have heard him say three healing words, "I love you." Without a doubt these times with God were acts of his divine grace to help me through what lay ahead, in my journey home.

Willingness

Ray was a powerful boy. He may have been the strongest fifth grader ever produced by a Franklin County elementary school. He had a large round face, buzz-cut hair, and arms the size of the back legs of a full-grown hog. He walked with a side-to-side saunter, like he was trying to stomp bugs on both sides of a hallway, as he progressed toward his prey. Nobody ever crossed Ray. He always got his way. If he wanted your new baseball, it was his; if he wanted your chocolate cupcake, his again.

Because of Ray's imposing physical size and his willingness to risk homicide charges, he was able to impose his will on his peers. He had great power and he always got what he wanted.

Tony Campolo, Jr., in his book, *The Power Delusion*, has a lot to say about folks like Ray, and the "Ray" inside each of us. He defines power as "the prerogative to determine what happens and the coercive force to make others yield to your wishes—even against their own will."[6] He says that his book is about power and the things people do to get it; and that he wrote it to show how a craving for power interferes with love and destroys personal relationships. He goes so far as to say that "the desire to be powerful interferes with the possibility of our being real Christians."

Campolo uses the word power in a way that is very similar to the way in which I use "behavioral narcotics." We both see it as a delusional substitute for the healing potency of love. He states the following. "It is love that heals. Troubled hearts and minds are made whole through his love. The physical body is restored through love. Ultimately, the entire universe will be healed by love (Rom 8:18-22)."[7] In the meantime, however, there is an incredible tendency to use power and willfulness instead of love to treat the fears and insecurities caused by compassion deficits. There is an incredible tendency to act like Ray and like the first Adam—seeking power and setting aside love—rather than act like the second Adam, Christ, who willingly set aside power and sought love.

In my own life, it wasn't long after Jesus had bathed me in grace and whispered about his love for me, that he asked me to become more willing, and less willful. He reminded me that there were many ways I was attempting to play power games with him like Ray had played with his weaker peers.

I became aware that my use of perfectionism and ridiculously high standards was a way to make others like and accept me; a way to manipulate him into accepting me. My manipulation and control of others, through vain praise or harsh humiliation, was a way of bullying them into positions and postures where I felt more secure. He was asking me to seek powerlessness in the midst of a world that worships power. He was asking me to treat my deepest fears, resentment, and insecurities with love and humility instead of power, works, and control. It was like asking Ray to become a Mennonite. It was like asking Peter to become a disciple. In my opinion, it was asking far too much.

Fears and Idols

In the allegory told at the beginning of this book, our Adam encounters a sea monster shortly after he has become willing to take his oars out of the water at the advice of his spiritual director. The creature that appears is of unusual composition. Like most of our fears, it only has substance if it is believed to be real. Adam manages to escape death as he appropriates faith and believes that his enemy is really an illusion.

The sea monster in our story was used to represent the deepest fears in Adam's heart—fears brought to the surface by

Adam's choice to be willing; fears that cried out for him to grab his oars—his behavioral narcotics—and return to his rowing, away from home.

I, too, have a deep, submerged fear. It's not a fear of spiders, snakes, or the dark—although I will admit that being locked in a pitch-black room in the company of things slimy or eight-legged would be no picnic. When I began to experiment with willingness and took my oars out of the water by turning away from self-sufficiency, I soon discovered that I was being pursued. My own personal sea monster was a deep-seated fear of abandonment. It may sound benign, but it was and is terrifying.

It is the horrified face of a three year old who has discovered he has been separated from his parents at a busy mall. It is the sight of your house engulfed in flames. It is the screams of a child who cries out from his crib to an empty house. It is the taillights of a moving van disappearing from view, carrying your best friend toward the opposite coast. It is all of these things rolled into one.

Now, none of these things actually happened to me, and I am not completely sure where my particular sea monster came from. It really doesn't matter. It predates my earliest memory, and I have spent my entire life trying to stay well out in front of it. I have done some pretty fast rowing to avoid this bogeyman. Apparently I began to rationalize at a very early age that I could do something to prevent being abandoned. I could be perfect.

I could set lofty, snow-capped goals and attain them. Then, surely, no one would ever abandon me. I would be too valuable to be left behind. And if some significant other ever did entertain such a notion, well, I could always use words—reason, argument, and criticism—as whips to make that person come back.

Winning the praise and respect of others, seeing nods of approval, feeling their pats on the back, these were my idols; and as long as I could see the nod, and feel the pat, I knew I was not alone. The most concrete idol I had was my resumé. It was a treasured listing of all the places my rowing had taken me. It was proof that I did not deserve to be rejected.

It was currency that I could cash in to satisfy the basic human drive for significance. After all, if you publish papers and intern at a major medical center, you are somebody. Right? Then there was security: of course you will get a fantastic job with a resumé like that. And it was pleasure: with that kind of a job can creature comforts be far behind?

But just in case the currency didn't work, I also had a sword—my tongue. If anyone dared not play the game of giving praise and respect and of promising not to leave, I could use words to stab them, to point out to them how anyone who refused to play my game must have a serious character flaw. And, I knew the *DSM*. I could prove it.

Serving my fears and worshiping my idols proved to be a very bifurcated way to live—the perfect, hardworking angel for those who would play my game, the perfect fiery-dart-throwing devil for those who would not.

My Own Personal Cross

I have long been convinced that one of the central manifestations of sin in twentieth-century people is our neurotic need for control. We feverishly seek to manipulate—to be in charge. Yet, for all of the controlling we attempt, we can never seem to control what matters most: our relationship with God, our marriage, our children's destiny, our career. The irony is that the more we clamor to be in charge, the more we squeeze the life out of everything that is precious to us. Our longings for significance and security are God-given, but how we seek to meet these needs often is not. Ignoring Jesus' mandate that he be glorified in our weaknesses, we try to glorify God in the worldliness of our strengths, by being in control. Sometimes God must allow us to be wounded before we can learn relinquishment.

Rebecca Manley Pippert, *The Power Delusion*

Rebecca's words proved to be very prophetic for my life. Not long after I consciously began to hang out with Jesus and to listen for his voice, I felt that I was hearing a consistent and repeated pattern in his communication with me. Soft, internal whispers and the flow of life's circumstances (what I call "parables-of-the-day"), seemed to be saying, "I love you. You can hardly fathom just how much. I will never leave nor forsake you. Trust me and become willing."

For quite some time the concepts of "willingness" (powerlessness and the surrender of control) and "willfulness" (maintaining white-knuckled control of all things of value in one's life) became an almost constant meditation. In my devotional times I pulled out a magnifying glass and traced the paths of these two threads as they were woven into the fabric of Scripture. It wasn't long before I had resolved with all my will, to become willing. The results were disastrous.

By the spring of 1984 I was ready to add the last two lines to my resumé—"Prestigious post-doctoral internship" and "Wonderful academic job associated with some later-to-be-named prestigious-sounding university." I had done all the right things—published papers, presented papers, won awards, landed one of the best pre-doctoral internships in the country, and I had become good friends with a mentor who promised he could get me into an eye-popping internship. And I had accomplished all this with most of my peers and professors thinking I was the most humble person since St. Francis. Well, at least since Festus of *Gunsmoke* fame. But there was no mistaking it, I was "hearing" the word "willingness." So I told the mentor no thanks and began to pencil in the revisions at the end of my vitae. I chose a far less prestigious second which offered the advantage of my being within walking distance of my wife and one-year-old daughter.

When it came time to apply for a job, I didn't. As I told you earlier in this book, instead of looking for work, I applied to live with the monks of the Taizé community in France. My wife and I were invited for a week-long interview, but our application was rejected. There was no place to check "MC" for married with children. So we ended up spending the first year after graduate school unemployed. We went through our savings faster than a Concord through France.

The highlights of that year were our forty visits to retreat centers all across the country and the thirty days I spent going through an Ignatian retreat somewhere in upstate New York. The "low-lights" of that year were being asked a thousand times, "Can't you get a job?" By the end of the year, the savings account hit "zero," and I felt like the inside of one.

In the years that followed, I opened a private practice in clinical psychology, and eventually took a job teaching in a not-quite-so-prestigious-as-I-had-once-envisioned graduate school for an initial salary that fell far short of what was needed to pay rent and student loans. Then, after my first year of teaching, things got really bad.

On an early-July morning, in the summer of 1989, I was leaving the house to go in to work teaching a summer session in an attempt to produce a balanced family budget. My wife was standing at the front door and I was a little surprised that she was seeing me off like June Cleaver. We had been fighting the night before. I don't remember what it was about. I don't think I knew then. She gave me a tender kiss on the cheek. Surprised again, I looked into her eyes and saw what appeared to be a deep sadness. I got into the car and backed out of the driveway and into the street.

For some reason I glanced back at the house. She was standing outside our front door. And even from the increasing distance of thirty, forty, fifty, one-hundred feet, I could still see that same look I had left in the doorway. It was a sad look—a very sad look. I got an eerie feeling in my stomach.

When I returned home that night, my wife and two young daughters were gone. There was a note on the table. In the note Jeanie carefully, gently, and lovingly explained that she could not live with me any longer. She didn't know when, or if, she could ever return. She wasn't divorcing me. She wasn't officially separating from me. She was saying and acting on the fact that I had become impossible to live with. Ever since I had been attempting willingness, I had become like a drug addict without his drugs, and to make matters worse, I hadn't been Prince Charming when I was "using."

For the next three weeks I spent most of my time lying on the floor in various rooms in our house crying until the carpet got soggy. When I wasn't doing that, I was teaching my classes, much like a zombie might do it, calling Jeanie and trying to manipulate her into coming back, or watching all the current-release movies, so that time would be more merciful in its passing. There wasn't a whole lot of eating or sleeping going on.

And sometimes I talked to God. I reminded him of all that I had done for him during the past five years. I made sure that he knew just how willing I had become. I asked him if it had slipped his mind that I had given up a prestigious internship for him; worked a solo-practice in rural Georgia for him; and had been teaching his future Christian counselors for a Denny's-managers-make-more-money-than-me salary … just for him.

Silence.

It wasn't until after I had come near to dehydration from all the tears I'd cried; not until I realized words were not going to bring my family back; not until I had coughed out most of my angry venom in God's direction, did he begin to talk. While I never heard an audible word, the following communication came through loud and clear.

"I love you. Nothing can ever change that. I delight in the time we spend together, and in your listening for my voice. Yes I desire for you to become willing—willing to trust and follow me. But so far, you and not I have decided just what that means. I choose what is most simple and mundane. I choose that you become willing to love your wife and children. I choose that you see me in the face of everyone who comes across your path."

He said more, but I'm a bit shy about attempting to turn inward whispers into words on paper.

Slowly, I began to realize that my choices of the past few years had been just—my choices. And, perhaps … no, definitely … I had simply begun to construct another resumé, a second idol. More specifically, it was a ledger sheet of how much God owed me, because of all that I had been *willing* to give up. I realized that becoming willing was something quite different from that, far more simple and mundane.

God wanted me to be willing to be available to the present moment, to my wife, children, and friends. He didn't want me to be focused on what I was giving up (status and power) but rather on what I could be gaining (life, and life in full).

Choosing not to further build a resumé was inconsequential. Choosing to take out the trash, read my children a story, stay up late listening to my wife, write a letter of encouragement to a friend, these things were of the highest consequence.

I once read that Ted Turner has a sign on his desk which reads, "Lead, follow, or get out of the way." Even after my attempts at willingness I had a similar sign on my forehead. It read, "Mentor, compliment, or get out of my way ... I'm trying to save my soul here."

Poor Jeanie, I thought. At least Ted found time to take Jane to a Braves game. I had been far too absorbed with the work of spiritual maturity for such amusements. Eventually, I saw the light. Eventually, the wounds of abandonment helped me to learn about relinquishment and about true, simple, mundane willingness. *His biggest fear.*

Before August arrived, so did Jeanie. She finally had a new husband, something like the one she must have thought she was getting years before. Because of her act of bravery, she became my hero.

Forgiveness

Smiley Blanton begins his book, *Love or Perish*, with these words.

Whatever you do in life, do it with love! We have no alternative save to act from motives of hate—yet how doleful to make this our choice! For hate [and fear] is the destroyer of life, where love is its guardian. Hate [and fear] blinds our vision and warps our talents; but love releases our energies for the creative action that sustains mankind ... [love] has tamed our savage nature and taught us how to transform a primitive wilderness into a cultivated garden (brackets mine).[8]

I wasn't quite there yet—the cultivated garden of Eden. But I finally had insight. There was an obstacle to my re-entering the garden—forgiveness.

In the movie *Ghandi* there is a powerful scene where Ghandi lies near death on the front porch of a house. A bearded man, a Hindu, comes to his side and pleads for help. He tells Ghandi that he has been living in hell for the past several days. He had witnessed the brutal murder of his two children at the hands of Muslims.

Ghandi tells him, with a weak but sure voice, that he knows a way out of hell. He tells the man that he must find two children that have been orphaned by the war. They must be the same age as were his own children. The man nods. But, says Ghandi, "They must be Muslim children." Color drains from the man's face and he swallows hard. "And," Ghandi continues, "you must raise them as Muslims."

The way out of hell is obviously very difficult, and almost always winds through the narrow pass of forgiveness. I thought long and hard about my need to forgive. It seemed quite irrational to forgive my parents. I knew they had always loved me with all their hearts.

There was nothing to forgive Jeanie. She had truly acted as a loving mother and wife. I would liked to have thought that it was my in-laws that needed forgiving. Lord knows it's easy to blame them when things go wrong. But that didn't feel right either.

I considered all the talk I had heard about people needing to forgive God. I searched for some buried hatred for him. After all, anyone with all those "omnis" in front of his name must bear some responsibility. But no, there was nothing to forgive him for, either.

The person I most needed to forgive was the last one I considered. It was me. I was the one in the driver's seat; the one calling all the shots; the one that couldn't recognize Jesus when he was sitting on my lap, asking for a second bedtime story. I told God that the one I needed to forgive was me. And do you know what God did? He sentenced me to the same fate handed out by Ghandi. I had to find a child just like me and love him like a Christian. I found that child in a surprising place. I found him in the mirror.

Reconciliation

The French theologian Pierre Teillard de Chardin (I love that name), observes that love is whatever unifies or brings things together. Consequently, it is love that creates the universe. Love that unifies protons and electrons into atoms, atoms into molecules, molecules into amino acids, and the whole mix into people. It is love that brings things together, love that heals, love that makes troubled minds and hearts whole. Love that brings all of us Adams back home. In the end, the entire universe will be healed by love (Rom 8:18-22).

Love is analogous to the powerful constructive energy of fusion; hate and fear to the nightmarishly destructive power of fission. It was love that brought me back home to the shores of Eden. But, I was in for one final surprise. I didn't recognize the God into whose arms I fell.

There is a story about a man named Melvin who decided to soften the blows of mid-life by making a lot of changes. He had one of his extra chins removed and his nose down-sized. He bought himself some contact lenses and had several rows of hair planted on the top of his shiny round head. He then went out and got some tight pants and an open-to-the-navel silk shirt, and squeezed the whole new package into a red Miata.

One day as he was pulling out into the street, a huge truck smashed into him-wrinkling both pants and his Miata. When he arrived in heaven, he was incredulous. He confronted God and asked with a very loud voice, "How come you let that truck hit me just when I felt good about living again?"

God said, "Melvin? Melvin Dinkins? Is that you!? I didn't recognize you!"

While I have not followed in the footsteps of Melvin, I came to realize that I had been constantly recreating God throughout my life. After a while, it became hard for me to recognize him. In the last lines of Tillich's book, *Courage To Be*,[9] he observes that it is a very different God who emerges from the tomb of our doubt and fears. A far bigger God.

At the end of my journey, at least this phase, I have discovered that my God, the God of my Sunday school, was very different from the God in whose arms I now rest.

The former God had arms that were far too short, a mind that was too distracted, and a heart that was sometimes cold. He was interested only in what I could *do*. The God of the Easter of my own personal cross, has arms that reach around the world, a mind that is single-focused, and a heart that is as warm as a campfire. He says, "Welcome home, my good and faithful servant. I am he who will never leave you nor forsake you." To which I say, "God, it's really you! I almost didn't recognize you."

I could go on and on, but the Bishop is banging at the door.

The End

Epilogue

A Few Questions and Answers Before You Go

It has been almost four years since I pecked out the words "The End" to conclude the five-year project of introspection you have just finished reading. I walked away from the bishop's quarters with the suspicion that whatever I had "ended" would remain a personal journal of confessions, observations, and ideas, locked away on hard drive.

During these last four years, however, I have not been able to resist printing out some of that material for use in a variety of classes and seminars. Captive audiences have included everyone from MTV-watching teenagers to retired missionaries, and from practicing psychologists to potential clients.

Along the way I ended up printing out so many copies that a local Kinkos put me on their Christmas list and started sending me thank you notes.

Recently, I was surprised. Editors from LifeSprings and Servant Publications began to talk to me about putting what you have just read into print. I became very excited. When they suggested a financial arrangement, I said, "I'll pay it!" When they said, "No, we'll pay you," I fainted.

In the passage of time between the writing of chapter seven and this epilogue, many people have conducted some holy experiments with the Eight Leaps. Because of this, it is now possible to share with you a few of their most repeated questions.

I present them in hope that they will increase the likelihood you will flip over to Appendix A and begin your own trial program in deep-sea navigation. There you will find suggestions for turning your local Bible, public library, video rental outlet, and music store into resources for personal and spiritual growth. But first the questions.

Are there only eight leaps involved in spiritual growth?

Oh my, no! I used Eight Leaps, in part, as a tip-of-the-hat to the wonderfully helpful "Twelve Step" programs. I believe that whether Christian spiritual growth is described in one step, eight leaps, or eighty triple-axles, if authentic, it will center upon the need for us to conform to the life and character of Christ. Such conformity comes about through cooperation with grace—the grace of having a live-in, conversing Christ. Trying to obey his voice and become less "me" and more "Jesus" could cause a person to leap about in an infinite number of directions.

I do, however, believe that these leaps represent eight off-ramps from the road to abundant life. That is, if a Christian is not fully alive to the peace and joy of being in God's kingdom, he or she may wish to examine these areas to see if a detour has been made.

With that said, I would suggest walking away from anyone who adamantly prescribes a definite and fixed formula for spiritual growth. If his or her recipe features words which all start with the same letter of the alphabet, shoot 'em in the foot before you leave.

Is the path of spiritual formation linear—
a straight line progression?

I think the path to spiritual maturity more often resembles the circular progressions of a "Slinky" than a straight line. It has been my experience that any given day brings with it opportunity for growth in each of the Eight Leaps. Wrestling with willingness, for example, may cause me to simultaneously stare at my "fears and idols" while praying for an increased sense of resting in God's presence.

Isn't all this just "getting saved?"

Yes and no. It's about salvation for the already saved. To be saved is to have the best fire insurance policy in the universe and to have room reservations for eternity. The Eight Leaps are about the process of spiritual transformation. Many who are "saved" from Egypt never cross the wilderness or pass into the here-and-now promised land. That takes a disciplined effort of cooperating with God's grace.

What's the deal with the Christian disciplines?

I can best answer that by telling you about William Barton, a minister, writer, and columnist. He had an extraordinary gift. Like his Master, Jesus, he was able to grasp the deepest spiritual truth, wrap it loosely in story, and hand it to a child for safekeeping in his heart. One of his stories, told by his alter ego, Safed the Sage, has changed my life.

Safed and his little granddaughter were walking together when tiny snowflakes began to fall from the sky. The little maiden became captivated by the sight and exclaimed, "Grandpa! Look how the snow falls in crumbs and bubbles."

Safed immediately began to marvel—more at his granddaughter's creative use of words than God's wondrous work with water. When he asked how it was that she chose the words, "crumbs and bubbles," she replied. "See? Some falls on your face and makes little bubbles. Some falls on your overcoat and becomes crumbs." Safed could not argue with

her description—apparently she had his own gift for pic-
turesque speech.

After their walk and after they had a long winter's nap, Safed
awoke to a neighborhood wrapped in total silence. He mar-
veled again, "How small were those crumbs and bubbles of
snow which fell on my face and coat. But now they have piled
up in such drifts that they stop mighty trains."

It is the "habits" of our life, the ways that we spend the
thousands of present moments we are given each day, that
determine our course and destination. Daily habits of self
absorption and over control will derail spiritual growth.
Whereas, the spiritual disciplines, mere "crumbs and bubbles"
taken one-by-one, can become a methodology for absorbing
the love in which we live.

The spiritual disciplines, simply put, are a variety of ways of
"hanging out" with God. The spiritual disciplines are like the
"crumbs" and "bubbles" in Safed's story, or the push-ups and
early morning laps of an athlete. Taken one-by-one their
impact is minuscule. But taken together, they can pile up and
stop a runaway ego.

Christian disciplines, according to Dallas Willard, are the
things we *can* do by direct effort which make it possible to do
the things we could never have done by direct effort. They can
be the occasion for being challenged concerning "leaps" of
faith and the methodology for being plugged into God's
love—so that we will have the energy for the jump.

*How do the Eight Leaps compare to other models
of transformation?*

For the Scientific-Minded

Rebecca Propst, in her landmark book, *Psychotherapy in a
Religious Framework: Spirituality in the Emotional Healing
Process*,[1] investigates numerous psychological and theological
models of change. She concludes that transformation in both
camps is built on the foundation of "relationship" and
"insight."

She then argues that all theological models of change add to
this foundation two pillars—the need for change in the areas
of: 1) gaining a renewed perspective on what we can be; and 2)
struggling to define ourselves according to the will of God.

I believe the Eight Leaps are a means of fleshing out
Propst's observations. The hermit (see chapter one), as with
the first three helpers offered relationship and insight. But the
relationship to which he points—practicing the presence of
God and learning to discern his voice—is, ostensibly, far more
powerful than what was offered by the first three helpers.
Additionally, his insight into Adam's pain—as being caused by
a spiritual homesickness—is also new and improved.

To this foundation the hermit suggested a new perspective
on how things can be and then prescribed "willingness." The
"leaps" that follow underscore how difficult it is to live in a
state of perpetual self-surrender.

For the Biblical-Minded

Nelson B. Baker, Ph.D., Emeritus Professor of English Bible
at Eastern Baptist Seminary, wrote *You Can Understand the
Bible*.[2] In the book he suggests that from any page of Scripture
you can look around and get a view of its unifying themes. I
will paraphrase below.

1. God desires to live in a loving relationship with his children and that they love each other.

2. He has prepared a wonderful inheritance for his special creation—humankind. The inheritance can be viewed as the Garden of Eden, the Promised Land, and the kingdom of Heaven.

 3. We blow it. Disbelief that God has our best interest at heart keeps us plotting our own course—keeps costing us enjoyment of the inheritance.

4. God offers a progressive means of restoration—Covenant, Law, his unfathomable love as manifest in the person of his Son and presence of the Holy Spirit.

   If nothing else works he releases the "hound of heaven."

I believe the Eight Leaps can be viewed as a way to conceptualize the journey back home—to a here-and-now enjoyment of the inheritance of his present kingdom. I believe they point to the grace of the Eden-like realization that we walk in the presence of our heavenly Father.

For the Historical-Minded

In the early centuries of church history the process of spiritual maturity was often described as entailing movements of "illumination," "purgation," and "transformation." Woven into the Eight Leaps is the need for:

1. Illumination—my soul is restless and at sea until it rests in God, until its will is aligned with the will of its creator;

2. Purgation—the aligning of human and divine will depends on two crosses—that of Jesus, and my own dying daily to the use of idols of pain management;

3. Transformation—the result of cooperating with God and avoiding the temptations of taking an "off-ramp."

For the Child-Minded

In addition to the above (which I fear may bore the children) I am intrigued by how well the discussions in this book line up with classic children's stories. Specifically, *The Wizard of Oz.*

In my early years of practice as a psychologist I began to feel a lot like the wizard who resided in Oz. After all, there was never a person who came to me for advice, who did not remind me of one of the characters of the classic.

Some, like the Scarecrow, needed work in the area of thought—cognitive restructuring, I had learned to call it. Some were more like the Tin Man—in need of a change of heart, of feeling. Lions came who needed to learn how to behave, to act, in a more courageous manner. And some came with an existential dilemma—how to be happy in their Kansas.

I often felt like the wizard, hiding behind a curtain and projecting a giant green head—an image of truth and wisdom, grounded more in smoke and mirrors than in sound theological reality. But many were helped. There is value in changing thoughts, feelings, and behaviors. There is value in taking the time to wrestle with one's witches.

I came to believe the way I practiced psychology bore a close resemblance to the making of the movie. But I began to wonder about the role of the true maker of lions, and tigers, and bears, and oh my! Yes! Of Dorothys, too!

Proposed in this book is a different script. I have suggested that the Maker is available, and that you can practice his presence and learn to hear his voice. I also have suggested that he longs to walk with you, right by your side, helping you fight your witches and sea monsters. He stays with you until the yellow bricks in your road turn to gold, and your black-and-white Kansas becomes a colorful kingdom—a land full of "Ahs!" And that's just the beginning, the now. The real kingdom is mostly for later.

Appendix A

Resources for Eight-Giant-Leaps Christian Formation Groups

LEAP ONE: THE KINGDOM OF GOD

POINTS TO PONDER

1. The "kingdom of God" is the central theme of the gospel message. The invitation to live a new life in the kingdom is *the* message. To understand its meaning is to understand who Jesus is and what he came to do. To misunderstand the kingdom is to misunderstand Jesus and his mission.

2. The concept of the kingdom is not just a New Testament phenomenon; it was all through the Old Testament, as well. Notice that Jesus never stopped to define it for the people. He knew they already understood what he was talking about. They just missed the point. John Bright, an Old Testament scholar, points out in his award-winning book *The Kingdom of God* that in the Old Testament the common understanding about the kingdom of God involved an expectancy of a recovery of the lost Eden. Bright also claims that the central theme in Scripture is **SALVATION TO LIFE IN THE KINGDOM.**

3. Dallas Willard, in his teaching-tape series on the kingdom (see third section below) says that Jesus did only three things while he was on earth.
- He announced the kingdom.
- He taught about its nature.
- He demonstrated his authority to do such announcing and teaching through miracles.

4. Eleven of the parables of Jesus are introduced with, "The kingdom is like … " Only sixty-six days of the life of Jesus are recorded in Scripture, yet he uses the word "kingdom" eighty times.

5. What is the kingdom of God? It is the sphere where God's rule is obeyed. It is the place where the rules of the King are the rules by which his subjects live their lives. To stay in Christ means to return home to the Kingdom and stay put.

SCRIPTURE TO CONSIDER

1. The kingdom was announced by Jesus.

> Jesus went throughout Galilee, teaching in their synagogues, preaching the good news of the kingdom, and healing every disease and sickness among the people (Matthew 4:23, NIV). See also Matthew 9:35; and Luke 4:43; 16:16.

2. Many of the parables contain lessons about the kingdom.

> Listen then to what the parable of the sower means: When anyone hears the message about the Kingdom and does not understand it, the evil one comes and snatches away what was sown in his heart…. But, the one who received the seed

that fell on good soil is the man who hears the word and understands it. He produces a crop, yielding a hundred, sixty, or thirty times what was sown (Matthew 13:18-23 NIV). See also Matthew 13:23-35; Mark 4:26-29; Luke 14:28-32.

3. The kingdom is a double reality; it is already here, yet it is to come in its fullness hereafter.

Then Jesus asked, "What is the kingdom of God like? What shall I compare it to? It is like a mustard seed, which a man took and planted in his garden. It grew and became a tree, and the birds of the air perched in its branches." Again He asked, "What shall I compare the kingdom of God to? It is like yeast that a woman took and mixed into a large amount of flour until it worked all through the dough" (Luke 13:18-21, NIV). See also Matthew 25:1-13.

4. Righteousness, peace, and joy are signs of the Kingdom given by the Father to his Son.

But seek first his Kingdom and his righteousness, and all these things will be given to you as well" (Matthew. 6:33, NIV). See also Luke 12:31; Romans 14:17; 1 Corinthians 15:24; Colossians 1:13.

USUAL AND UNUSUAL RESOURCES

1. The Kingdom of God, by John Bright. Its 27th printing was in 1990. It is published by Abingdon Press (Nashville).

2. The Gospel of the Kingdom of Heaven, by Dallas Willard. This is an audiotape series available through First Presbyterian Church of Hollywood (1760 North Gower Street, Hollywood,

CA 90028). Dr. Willard is presently working on a book on the kingdom. It is tentatively titled *The Kingdom Among Us* and should be available by late 1997.

3. The Cave. This is the video referred to in this book. It is available through Churchill Films (662 North Robertson Boulevard, Los Angeles, California 90069-9990). See also the description in chapter one.

4. Tales of the Kingdom, by David and Karen Mains. A wonderful collection of true fables about the kingdom. It is published by Chariot Books (Elgin, Illinois).

5. Tell Me the Secrets, by Max Lucado. Published by Crossway Books (Wheaton, Illinois).

ACTIVITIES—GROUP AND HOMEWORK

Group:

1. Reflect on those things that are more important in your life than seeking life in the kingdom. Then discuss why they are getting more than their share of your attention.

2. Discuss how your daily "Rule-of-Life" (the things you will definitely do each day) places you in greater awareness of the kingdom, as opposed to the world.

3. Read the "Walkin' Catfish" story (see chapter two) as a discussion starter concerning how natural, or unnatural it seems to be "Livin' in the Kingdom."

Show *The Cave* as a prelude to group discussion.

Homework

1. Sit under a tree with any old, classic fairy tale you read as a child. Read it again and then ask yourself if it is possible that it is a view of reality that is more real than Wall Street, or the tree you are leaning against. Ask God what your place is in his true fairy tale—the kingdom.

2. Get copies of *Tales of the Kingdom* and *Tell Me the Secrets*. Read them. But don't tell your children, if you have them. They'll want to hear them, too.

LEAP TWO: PRACTICING THE PRESENCE OF GOD

POINTS TO PONDER

1. In the Old Testament, God is frequently addressed as "Father" and Israel as his first-born son. In the New Testament the believer becomes an adopted son of God (Romans 8:15; Galatians 4:6). Jesus often refers to "Father," sometimes saying: "My Father" or "Your Father," and once: "My Father and your Father" (John 20:17). Paul even refers to God as "*Abba*," or "Daddy." Most dads like to hang out with their kids.

2. Arguably, the most cherished Sacrament in the Christian Church is the practice of the presence of God during the Eucharist (Lord's Supper). Regardless of what is believed about it in "actuality," all Christians see it as a reminder of the indwelling presence of Christ.

3. If in fact "Compassion Deficits" (see pages 4-41 and 188-190 of this book) are an underlying source of much psychological pain, doesn't it seem logical that one of the better

antidotes would be practicing the presence of Divine love—
God?

4. What is distinct about God's people is that he is in their
presence.

SCRIPTURE TO CONSIDER

1. God's love is all-embracing.

For the Lord your God is a merciful God; he will not abandon or destroy you or forget the covenant with your fore-
fathers, which he confirmed to them by oaths (Deute-
ronomy 4:31, NIV). See also Matthew 6:26-28 and
26:26-30; Luke 6:35; Acts 10:34.

2. Love is man's response to God's love for him.

"Teacher, which is the greatest commandment in the Law?"
Jesus replied: "'Love the Lord your God with all your heart
and with all your soul and with all your mind.' This is the
first and greatest commandment. And the second is like it:
'Love your neighbor as yourself'" (Matthew 22:36-39,
NIV). See also Mark 12:29-30; Luke 10:27; Romans 13:10;
1 John 3:14.

3. Nothing can separate us from God's love.

Then Jesus came to them and said, "All authority in heaven
and on earth has been given to me. Therefore go and make
disciples of all nations, baptizing them in the name of the

Father, and of the Son and of the Holy Spirit, and teaching them to obey everything I have commanded you. And surely I am with you always, to the very end of the age" (Matthew 28:18-20, NIV).

For I am convinced that neither death nor life, neither angels nor demons, neither the present nor the future, nor any powers, neither height nor depth, nor anything else in all creation, will be able to separate us from the love of God that is in Christ Jesus our Lord. (Romans 8:38-39, NIV).

See also Psalm 139; Luke 24:13-35; John 14:23; John 15; 1 Corinthians 6:19-20; Colossians 1:26-29.

4. God is also present in others.

When the Son of Man comes in his glory, and all the angels with him, he will sit on his throne in heavenly glory. All the nations will be gathered before him, and he will separate the people one from another as a shepherd separates the sheep from the goats. He will put the sheep on his right hand and the goats on his left. Then the King will say to those on his right, "Come, you who are blessed by my Father; take your inheritance, the kingdom prepared for you since the creation of the world. For I was hungry and you gave me something to eat, I was thirsty and you gave me something to drink, I was a stranger and you invited me in, I needed clothes and you clothed me, I was sick and you looked after me, I was in prison and you came to visit me" (Matthew 25:31-36, NIV).

USUAL AND UNUSUAL RESOURCES

1. God Views. This is a movie (videotape) written and performed by a professional actor, Kurt Cloninger. In it he explores several of our misconceptions about God. Is God a cosmic sheriff? A senile old man? A waiter at a four-star restaurant? Is he a hyperactive shop foreman, concerned only with what you may produce for him? Or, is he the prodigal son's father? These are the subjects of the production that was referenced in the book on page 197. It should still be available through: Straight to the Heart, P.O. Box 2352, Duluth, Georga, 30136.

2. The Practice of the Presence of God. By Brother Lawrence. Available through Whitaker House (Springdale, PA).

3. Prayer: Finding the Heart's True Home. By Richard Foster. Available through Harper, San Francisco. See especially chapters 12-14 (prayer of the heart, meditative prayer, and contemplative prayer).

4. Love You Forever. By Robert Munsch. Firefly Books (Willowdale, Ontario).

5. Discovering God through the Daily Practice of His Presence. By Anthony M. Coniaris. Available through Light and Life Publishing Company. P.O. Box 26421, Minneapolis, Minnesota 55426.

ACTIVITIES FOR GROUP AND HOMEWORK

Group:
1. Show *God Views* in its entirety. (It will take about thirty-five minutes.) Lead a discussion concerning misperceptions of God, and how those misperceptions leave us with a God whose presence we would want to avoid, not practice.

2. Rent *The Little Prince* from a nearby video store. Preview the section where the prince is learning how to tame the fox. Show this section to the group (approximately ten minutes) and discuss similarities and dissimilarities to our developing relationship to God in prayer.

3. Read *Love You Forever* to the group. When you have finished, after you stop crying, have the group discuss how it would affect them to believe, truly believe, that they are loved that much by God.

4. Play a selection from a "praise and worship" CD of your choice which calls to mind the here-and-now presence of God. Allow several minutes of silent meditation after the song ends.

Homework:
1. Take several blank sheets of paper and draw the most heretical view of God you have ever held. Then ask yourself if there is still anything from that view that makes it difficult for you to come into God's presence.

2. Now draw what you know to be a truthful picture of God. Put it on the refrigerator door for a week as a reminder of the One in whose presence you reside.

3. Begin reading Foster's book on prayer, *Prayer: Finding the Heart's True Home.*

4. Begin reading *Celebration of Discipline*, also by Richard Foster.

LEAP THREE: HEARING GOD

POINTS TO PONDER

1. Imagine that you are a youth-league basketball coach and that you have just won first prize in a contest. As a result, Dean Smith (head basketball coach for the University of North Carolina) will be flown to your house each morning to be your private tutor. Now imagine that he has fulfilled his part of the deal for several weeks. He has been present in your living room. But he hasn't been able to teach you much because you have been doing all the talking. Does your prayer life ever resemble this picture—being in the presence of the ultimate coach in the universe, Jesus, only to discover that you have seldom stopped to listen to his advice? (See page 164 of the book.)

2. If taken to the extreme, intercessory prayer can reduce God to a divine butler. If taken to the extreme, listening prayer can turn God into a counselor, and us into his friends.

3. The practice of solitude and silence are the prerequisite Christian disciplines for the development of listening prayer.

4. Which is more important—the author or the book?

5. How can we find God's will for our lives if we don't ask?

SCRIPTURE TO CONSIDER

1. According to Peter Lord, in his book *Hearing God,* one of the primary teachings of the New Testament is that "God the Holy Spirit lives in the believer now, to be to the believer all that Jesus was to the disciples. This was one of Jesus' greatest promises" (p. 14).

> And I will ask the Father, and he will give you another Counselor to be with you forever — the spirit of truth … you will know him, for he lives with you and will be in you (John 14-17, NIV).

> For you did not receive a spirit that makes you a slave again to fear, but you received the Spirit of sonship. And by him we cry, "Abba, Father." The Spirit testifies with our spirit that we are God's children (Romans. 8:15-16, NIV).

2. Being able to hear God implies that we practice his presence, living in a state where we "abide" in him.

> As for you, the anointing you received from him remains [abides] in you, and you do not need anyone to teach you. But as his anointing teaches you about all things and as that anointing is real, not counterfeit—just as it has taught you, remain in him (1 John 2:27, NIV).

> Remain in me, and I will remain in you. No branch can bear fruit by itself; it must remain in the vine. Neither can you bear fruit unless you remain in me (John 15:4, NIV).

3. God's sheep know his voice.

The watchman opens the gate for him, and the sheep listen to his voice. He calls his own sheep by name and leads them out. When he has brought out all his own, he goes on ahead of them, and his sheep follow him because they know his voice. But they will never follow a stranger; in fact, they will run away from him because they do not recognize a stranger's voice (John 10:3-5, NIV).

USUAL AND UNUSUAL RESOURCES

1. *Hearing God*, by Peter Lord. It is published by Baker Book House (Grand Rapids, Michigan).

2. *Listening Prayer*, by Leanne Payne. This is Leanne's latest book (published in late 1994). It is published by a division of Baker Books.

3. *Tell Me the Secrets*, by Max Lucado. Crossway Books (Wheaton, Illinois). See "The Song of the King." It is a story within the story, "Victory."

4. *In Search of Guidance*, by Dallas Willard. It is published by Zondervan/Harper Collins.

5. *The Will of God*, by Leslie D. Weatherhead. It is published by Abingdon Press (Nashville, Tennessee).

ACTIVITIES FOR GROUP AND HOMEWORK

Group:
1. Read "The Song of the King" story to the group. Have them discuss the implications for their lives. (See *Tell Me the Secrets.*)

2. Read page 140 from this book to the group (or, better yet have them read chapters seven through eleven of *Hearing God* as a homework activity) and then lead a discussion about the dynamics of tuning in to WGOD instead of WSIN.

3. Have the group practice a few moments of "attentive silence" before each member asks God, "What do you think of me?" Allow sharing if anyone desires.

4. Provide instructions concerning the basics of keeping a personal prayer journal.

Homework:
1. Pass out photocopies of a "week-at-a-glance" calendar. Have the group members find a ten-minute block of time on each weekday, during which they can spend time listening to God. Have each group member commit to spending those ten minutes each day, sitting in God's presence and listening to his voice. Again, it will be much better if they have purchased a copy of *Hearing God*, and read chapters seven through eleven, before doing this activity.

2. After practicing the above for a week, suggest to the group that they continue the activity with a pencil and notebook (journal) in their laps. Request that they develop the habit of jotting down any broadcasts they have heard from WGOD.

3. After another week has passed, make the suggestion that

they begin to use Peter Lord's grid to help sort out the voice of God from that of WSIN and WSELF.

4. Read the book of Hosea (at one sitting) as a reminder of the depth and breadth of God's love.

LEAP FOUR: WILLINGNESS VERSUS WILLFULNESS

POINTS TO PONDER

1. Willingness implies a surrender of our separateness from God, and entrance into his will on a day-to-day, hour-by-hour, moment-by-moment basis. It is saying yes to God's divine whisper (which we "hear" while practicing his presence) several hundred times daily.

2. Willfulness implies setting oneself apart from God (in effect from the fundamental essence of life) in an attempt to master, direct, control, or otherwise manipulate our existence.

3. More simply, willingness is saying yes to the mystery of being alive as a Christian, in each moment. Willfulness is saying "no," or perhaps more commonly, "Yes, but ... "

4. If grace is seen as all that God can do, willingness is seen as all that we can do. When both are active, life can become abundant.

5. Whereas psychology is fundamentally objective and secular and often promotes willfulness, the core identity of religion is mysterious and spiritual. It promotes willingness.

6. Have you ever had a positive religious experience which did not involve a willing surrender?

7. Willingness is not passivity or non-assertiveness. It is saying with Mary on the hillside and Jesus in the garden, "Your will and not mine be done."

8. We, like the children of Israel in the wilderness and the congregates in Paul's first-century churches, struggle with the choice between willingness and willfulness on a daily basis.

SCRIPTURAL SCENES TO CONSIDER CONCERNING THE BATTLE BETWEEN WILLINGNESS AND WILLFULNESS

1. God telling Adam, " … You are free to eat from any tree in the garden; but you must not eat from the tree of the knowledge of good and evil. For when you eat of it you will surely die" (Genesis 2:16-17).

2. The willful examples of the builders of the Tower of Babel. " … Come let us build ourselves a city, with a tower that reaches into the heavens, so that we may make a name for ourselves and not be scattered over the face of the whole earth" (Genesis 11:4).

3. Abraham's willingness to sacrifice his very own son. (Genesis 22:9).

4. Moses being told to throw down his rod (his symbol of self-protection) in the presence of his enemy (Pharaoh). As it turned out, as a device for self-protection it was really a serpent (Exodus 7:6).

5. The children of Israel's willingness to leave Egypt. The willfulness that kept them in the wilderness for forty years.

6. Moses' willing (albeit reluctant) leading of the exodus, yet, willful dealings with a rock (Exodus 17:1-7).

7. David's willingness to go out and fight Goliath (1 Samuel 17) and willful disobedience with Bathsheba (2 Samuel 11).

8. The same willing and willful king writing … "The Lord is my shepherd, I shall not want" (Psalm 23).

9. The exhortation to willingness which was at the heart of most of the major and minor prophets … spoken to address willfulness (apple-eating behavior).

10. A young Jewish girl, after being told by an angel that she would conceive a baby, as a virgin, says "I am the Lord's servant … May it be to me as you have said … " (Luke 1:38).

11. The temptation of Jesus, which is passed by his proclaiming that his will is not for food, or power, or immortality, but to do the will of his father (Luke 4:1-12).

12. Jesus' disciples willingly leave everything to follow Jesus. He insists on it (Luke 5:1-15).

13. Judas breaks the pack by willfully asserting that his own will not Jesus' will be done. It's a choice that leaves him swinging from a tree (Luke 22).

14. Jesus teaches, when teaching his disciples how to pray, that they should start their conversations with his Father with the

words: "Our Father who art in heaven, ... Thy will be done'"(Luke 22:41, 42).

15. Jesus in the garden. "He withdrew about a stone's throw beyond them, knelt down and prayed, 'Father, if you are willing, take this cup from me; yet not my will, but yours be done'" (Luke 22:39). He punctuated this with obedience unto death.

16. Paul's willing submission to the will of God, even through imprisonment, numerous beatings, and difficult travels.

17. The willfulness of the Christians in the churches Paul established—a willfulness which made it necessary for him to write a significant chunk of the New Testament.

USUAL AND UNUSUAL RESOURCES

1. *Will & Spirit: A Contemplative Psychology,* by Gerald G. May, M.D. Published by Harper & Row.

2. *The Millionaire and the Scrub Lady and Other Parables,* by William E. Barton. Published by Zondervan (Grand Rapids).

3. *Love You Forever,* by Robert Munsch. Published by Firefly Books (Willodale, Ontario).

4. *The Giving Tree,* by Shel Silverstein, Harper Collins Publisher.

5. *Improving Your Serve: The Art of Unselfish Living,* by Charles Swindoll. Published by Word, Incorporated, 1981.

ACTIVITIES FOR GROUP AND HOMEWORK

Group:
1. Read the "buckboard and reindeer" section from pages 169-172. Then read the "points to ponder" listed above and see where the discussion goes.

2. Read the "Crumbs and Bubbles" parable (pages 217-218) from *The Millionaire and the Scrub Lady*. Lead a discussion concerning the habits of our life (habits of willingness or willfulness) which are "crumbs and bubbles" that can pile up in such number that they can "stop a train."

Read the children's story *Love You Forever*. Discuss how believing in a God who is loving is the requisite for giving willing surrender a real chance in our lives.

Homework:
1. Recount a sincere experience with God that resulted in a willing surrender to his will. Fill a few journal pages with what happened in the ensuing days and weeks. How long was it before there was a temptation to cross your fingers when singing "He is Lord"?

2. Make a list of all your obstacles to willingness.

3. For the next week, every time you swallow any liquid, pray silently, "Not my will but yours be done."

4. Recount and list the costs for willfulness.

LEAP FIVE: OVERCOMING FEARS AND IDOLS

POINTS TO PONDER

1. If perfect love is able to cast out fear, it is perhaps reasonable to assume that perfect fear casts out love. After all, fear and love are physiological opposites; just as one cannot breathe shallowly and deeply at the same time, one cannot feel intense fear and intense love simultaneously.

2. In the absence of love and in the presence of fear, it is very human to look for God, or perhaps most often, God substitutes—idols. In the Judeo-Christian context, "idolatry" is defined as the worship of anything besides God, the Supreme Being of the universe, who is immortal, ultimate, transcendent, and imminent.

3. Neo-Freudian Erich Fromm said that the history of mankind is primarily the history of idol worship, from primitive idols of clay and wood to the modern idols of state, leaders, production, and consumption (from his book, *You Shall Be Gods*).

4. In essence an idol is anything that is given ultimate value and worshiped in place of God, the Holy One. According to Frederick Beuchner, "Idolatry is the practice of ascribing absolute value to things of relative worth (from *Wishful Thinking: A Theological ABC*).

5. According to G.K. Chesterton, "When we cease to worship God, we do not worship nothing, we worship anything." It must have been a Chesterton paraphrase when Bob Dillon set to music the words, "You've got to serve somebody."

6. Idols are created by people of faith as well as by non-believers. Their worship begins with the attempt to avoid pain (most often the pain of fear and loneliness) and ends with the refusal to turn from the idol which has been created to bow before God. At this point the idol, or pseudo god, has become an object of central passion, a craving for power, possession, or fame.

SCRIPTURE TO CONSIDER

God wastes no time in issuing commands against idol worship. The first of the Ten Commandments reads:

I am the Lord your God, who brought you out of Egypt, out of the land of slavery. You shall have no other gods before me. You shall not make for yourself an idol in the form of anything in heaven above or on the earth beneath or in the waters below. You shall not bow down to them or worship them; for I the Lord your God, am a jealous God, punishing the children for the sin of the fathers to the third and fourth generation of those who hate me, but showing love to a thousand generations of those who love me and keep my commandments.

Exodus 20:2-6, NIV

1. Yet, this commandment is broken before it is even brought down from the mountain—and the rest of the Old Testament is peppered with scores of instances where Israel (individually or collectively) breaks the most basic commandment.

2. Jesus reiterates the first of the Ten Commandments as primary, but rephrases it in terms of love. Jesus replied: "'Love the Lord your God with all your heart and with all your soul

and with all your mind.' This is the first and greatest commandment" (Matthew 22:37-38, NIV).

3. The final exam of Jesus in the wilderness was about resisting the temptation of idol worship. His essay answer was: "Away from me, Satan! For it is written: 'Worship the Lord your God, and serve him only.'"

4. The Gospels contain many stories and parables about fears and idols:
• "The rich young ruler" (Matthew 19:16-24; Mark 10:17-23; Luke 18:18-25).
• "The sower and the soils" (Mark 4:19).
• "The unrighteous Steward" (Luke 16:1-14).
• "The rich fool" (Luke 12:20).

5. In the first and second letter to the Corinthians, Paul repeatedly gives the instruction to run from idolatry and any form of immorality (see for examples 1 Corinthians 5:10-11; 6:9-13; 10:7, 14).

6. With the last line of his first letter, John warns the church to guard against idols "Dear children, keep yourselves from idols" (1 John 5:21, NIV).

USUAL AND UNUSUAL RESOURCES

1. Shattering the Gods Within: Victory Over the Powers that Control Us. David Allen, M.D. (Chicago: Moody Press).

2. You Shall Be As Gods. Erich Fromm (New York: Henry Holt).

3. Love Hunger. Minirth, F., Meier, P., Hemfelt, R., Sneed, S., & Hawkins, D. (New York: Fawcett Columina Publishers).

4. When I Relax I Feel Guilty. Tim Hansel (Chariot/Victor Books, 1979).

5. The Workaholic and His Family: An Inside Look. Minirth, F., Meier, P., Wichern, F., Brewer, B., & Skipper, S. (Grand Rapids: Baker Bookhouse)

ACTIVITIES FOR GROUP AND HOMEWORK

Group:
1. Show excerpts from the video, *Little Shop of Horrors*, in which a plant (the idol) makes a fearful man (Rick Moranis) rich and famous, but at the price of his life.

2. Show excerpts from the video, *Chariots of Fire.* This is a true story about an Olympic runner during the 1924 Olympic games who refuses to participate in any games on Sunday because it's the Lord's Day—he resists the lure of worldly idols.

3. Read the story "Chicken Little" (this can be found in W. J. Bennett's Ed., *The Book of Virtues: A Treasury of Great Moral Stories.* Ask the group to comment on the theme of fear idols found in the story.

4. Read the book *Is It Success? Or is it Addiction?*, by Pike, T. and Proctor, W. (Nashville: Thomas Nelson) and lead a discussion on how success can produce a cult lifestyle—which may be accepted by the church.

5. Play the song "No Other" (written by Donna Douglas and Margaret Becker, from the *Along the Road* album by Ashton, Becker, and Dente). Allow the group to meditate on the words for a few minutes before leading a discussion of "fears and idols."

Homework:

1. Give the group a take-home test of "Idol Assessment." You can make up your own items. The following suggestions are offered:

• How do you spend the majority of your time?
• When your mind wanders, what do you think about?
• What do you cherish most?
• If this (your most cherished object) were suddenly taken away, what would you feel? What makes you feel significant?
• What is your top priority in life?
• When you feel bad (fearful, depressed, lonely), to what do you turn for relief?
• What do you fear most? and how do you avoid this happening?
• Offer a group discussion the following week.

2. Have the class watch videos such as *Doc Hollywood*, or *Regarding Henry*, during the week and be prepared to lead a discussion during the next group meeting.

3. Assign the following passages of Scripture to be read between group meetings.
• Matthew 4:4   *Man does not live on bread alone ...*
• Matthew 11:28-30   *Come to me, all you who are weary ...*
• Matthew 19:16-30   *The rich young ruler ...*
• Matthew 22:37-39   *Love the Lord your God ...*

• Hebrews 13:5-6   *Keep your lives free from the love*
                     of money ...

LEAP SIX: OUR PERSONAL CROSS

POINTS TO PONDER

1. Embracing willingness brings us in close contact with our deepest fears and most cherished idols (see chapters three through six). At this point the would-be disciple of Christ has two options—return to willfulness (treating our fears with idol worship) or the acceptance of the pain of our own personal cross.

2. The cross of Jesus seemed ever on the mind of the apostle Paul. In fact, the Cross with all its offensiveness, became for Paul the uniting theme of the new faith. As he wrote to the Corinthians, "For I resolved to know nothing while I was with you except Jesus Christ and him crucified (1 Corinthians 2:2, NIV).

3. He regarded Christ's cross as the ultimate complete expression of obedience to God. Whereas Adam had wanted to be like God, Jesus, "Who, being in very nature God, did not consider equality with God something to be grasped ... And being found in appearance as a man, he humbled himself and became obedient to death—even death on a cross" (Philippians 2:6, 8, NIV).

4. We are to be imitators of Christ. The cross, with the pain it symbolizes, represents the ultimate in radical obedience. It is here, for the imitator of Christ, that willfulness is defeated and idols are smashed. To turn from it, as is so easy to do, is to turn

from the promises of authentic Christianity and of Easter morning to the realities of nominal Christianity and the thunderous darkness of Good Friday.

5. At the foot of our own personal cross is the intersection of the crossroads that lead to "life-in-full" or life-in-fear.

SCRIPTURE TO CONSIDER

1. Jesus insisted that all his followers should take up the cross.
" ... and anyone who does not take his cross and follow me is not worthy of me" (Matthew 10:38, NIV).

Then he called the crowd to him along with his disciples and said: "If anyone would come after me, he must deny himself and take up his cross and follow me" (Mark 8:34, NIV).

And anyone who does not carry his cross and follow me cannot be my disciple (Luke 14:27, NIV).

2. It is through acceptance of the cross of Jesus and our own personal cross that we find our true self, and life itself.

Whoever finds his life will lose it, and whoever loses his life for my sake will find it (Matthew 10:39, NIV).

For whoever wants to save his life will lose it, but whoever loses his life for me and for the gospel will save it (Mark 8:35, NIV).

3. The radical following of Christ is meant to lead to perfect union with him, crucified.

If we have been united with him like this in his death, we will certainly also be united with him in his resurrection. For we know that our old self was crucified with him so that the body of sin might be done away with, that we should no longer be slaves to sin—because anyone who has died has been freed from sin (Romans 6:5-7, NIV).

USUAL AND UNUSUAL RESOURCES

1. *Everyone's Way of the Cross,* by Clarence Enzler. (Notre Dame, Indiana: Ave Maria Press). This devotional book is a contemporary version of the traditional "Stations of the Cross."

2. *Revelations of Divine Love,* by Julian of Norwich. (Image books).

3. *Let Go,* by Francis Fenelon. (Whitaker House Publishers)

4. *No Wonder They Call Him the Savior,* by Max Lucado. (Multnomah Books).

5. *The Way of the Wolf,* by Martin Bell. (Seabury Press). See particularly the story entitled, "Barrington Bunny," the song "The Secret of the Stars," and the poem "Noel–The Lone Ranger."

ACTIVITIES FOR GROUP AND HOMEWORK

Group:
1. Have the group view the "crucifixion" scenes from the video, *The Lion, the Witch, and the Wardrobe.* Allow a group discussion to follow.

2. Read selections from *God Came Near—Chronicles of the Christ,* by Max Lucado (pages 49-52, 77-82, or 87-90 are recommended). Allow discussion.

3. View the crucifixion scenes from the video, *Jesus of Nazareth.* Ask the group to consider their willingness to have the idols of their lives nailed to a cross.

4. Lead a discussion on the "costs of non-crucified" living.

Homework:
1. Assign selected stories from *A Cry in the Wilderness.* This is a collection of stories and preaching by Keith Green. It is available through Sparrow Press. Encourage journaling around the issue of accepting personal crosses and the willingness to die to ourselves.

2. Encourage weekly journaling with any of the group activities listed above.

3. Have group members listen to meaningful music (such as "Lamb of God," performed by Twila Paris, or "The Cross Is a Radical Thing," performed by Steve Camp) and follow the experience by a time of quiet, listening-prayer.

LEAP SEVEN: FORGIVENESS

POINTS TO PONDER

1. To forgive means, "to give up resentment against or the desire to punish; stop being angry with; pardon; to cancel or remit a debt" (Webster).

2. To not forgive means that we are in a position where it is logistically impossible to keep the two supreme commandments of Christ—to love God with our whole being and to love all our neighbors as ourselves.

3. Many want to go forward with Christ while holding on to their anger and resentments with white knuckles. But it is impossible to hug God and neighbor with open arms and open palms while holding on to white-hot coals of bitterness—plus the coals are burning holes in the flesh and psyche of the one who will not let go.

4. With the possible exceptions of the kingdom of God, and love, one would be hard pressed to find a scriptural theme which receives more attention—a combination of total words and emphasis—than forgiveness. Perhaps this is because life in the "kingdom," and living in love has forgiveness as an entry way.

5. True forgiveness is never easy to accomplish. Most of us stop short (see pages 182-183 for a discussion on premature and post-mature forgiveness).

SCRIPTURE TO CONSIDER

1. There is no limit to forgiveness.

> Then Peter came to Jesus and asked, "Lord, how many times shall I forgive my brother when he sins against me? Up to seven times?" Jesus answered, "I tell you, not seven times, but seventy-seven times" (Matthew 18:21, 22, NIV).

2. Forgiveness by God calls for our willingness to forgive.

"Forgive us our debts, as we also have forgiven our debtors" (Matthew 6:12, NIV, see also Luke 11:4).

3. Jesus asks us to forgive.

Therefore, if you are offering your gift at the altar and there remember that your brother has something against you, leave your gift there in front of the altar. First go and be reconciled to your brother; then come and offer your gift (Matthew 5:23-24, NIV).

4. On the cross Jesus taught the lesson of forgiveness.

Jesus said, "Father, forgive them, for they do not know what they are doing." And they divided up his clothes by casting lots (Luke 23:34, NIV).

5. Paul stresses the necessity of our forgiving others.

Be kind and compassionate to one another, forgiving each other, just as in Christ God forgave you (Ephesians 4:32, NIV).

Bear with each other and forgive whatever grievances you may have against one another. Forgive as the Lord forgave you (Colossians 3:13, NIV).

USUAL AND UNUSUAL RESOURCES

1. For the individual who has struggled greatly to forgive and finds it an almost impossible task, the book, *The Return of the Prodigal Son*, by Henri Nouwen may be helpful. The following is a quote from the book:

I cannot forgive myself. I cannot make myself feel loved. By myself I cannot leave the land of my anger. I cannot bring myself home nor can I create communion on my own. I can desire it, hope for it, wait for it, yes, pray for it. But my true freedom I cannot fabricate for myself. That must be given to me. I am lost. I must be found and brought home by the shepherd who goes out to me. The story of the prodigal son is the story of a God who goes searching for me and who doesn't rest until he has found me. He urges and he pleads. He begs me to stop clinging to the powers of death and to let myself be embraced by arms that will carry me to the place where I will find the life I most desire (p. 82).

2. *The Mission* contains a powerful scene on forgiveness. The weight, or burden, of an unforgiving heart, the inability to forgive oneself in this case, is dramatically portrayed. The burden is finally "cut loose" by another. (Please see pages 181-182 for further descriptions).

3. The movie, *Ghandi*, while not a Christian movie, contains a poignant scene which provides unforgettable images of what is sometimes required of the forgiver, to experience peace. (See scene where a Hindu man comes to Ghandi for advice concerning how to be free from the "hell" of his anger—subsequent to the murder of his children by a Moslem. Ghandi assures him that there is a way out of hell, but he will have to find two Moslem children who have been orphaned, and raise them as Moslems.)

4. The opening parable of Lewis Smedes' book, *Forgive and Forget*, will be helpful in describing what can be the long and slow process of forgiveness.

5. See pages 182-183 of this book for description of Arch Hart's two-by-four analogy concerning how to avoid premature and post-mature forgiveness.

ACTIVITIES FOR GROUP AND HOMEWORK

Group:
1. Read the story, "A Girl Named Dirty," found in David and Karen Mains' book, *Tales of the Kingdom*. It is a the tale of a girl who finds acceptance and forgiveness from the King.

2. Consider excerpts from *The Ragamuffin Gospel*, by Brennan Manning. This book brings "good news" for the bedraggled, beat-up, and burnt out. It conveys deep realization of God's acceptance, forgiveness, and grace.

3. Consider showing "clips" from *The Mission*, and *Ghandi*, described above. Also consider reading the opening parable from *Forgive and Forget*.

4. Excerpts from *Return to the Aucas*—the story of Elizabeth Elliot's return mission trip to the very tribe who killed her husband—may be helpful.

Homework:
1. Certain group members may find it helpful to read *Making Peace with Your Parents*. This is a very practical book dealing with the journey from resentment toward parents to forgiveness.

2. *Amazing Love*, by Corrie ten Boom, and *May I Hate God?* by Pierre Wolff.

3. Slow-reading and journaling time with Emily Dickinson's poem, "After Great Pain, a Formal Feeling Comes."

4. Slow-listening and journaling to songs such as "Remember Not," on the CD *Susan Ashton,* by Susan Ashton. And for the "more secular" crowd, "The Living Years," on the CD *Living Years,* by Mike and the Mechanics.

5. Scenes from the movie *Les Miserables,* as a lead into personal journaling.

LEAP EIGHT: RECONCILIATION

POINTS TO PONDER

1. Ever since Adam fell and was expelled, man and God have been working on two endeavors—helping man to stand and to be reunited.

2. Ralph P. Martin, the prominent New Testament scholar, makes the case in his book, *Reconciliation,* that "reconciliation" is the "leading theme" or "center" of the New Testament message.

3. Martin goes on to conclude that "Paul's teaching on redemption is quite unintelligible except in the light of this universal longing (that we all have) for some scheme of cosmic salvation from these 'principalities and powers' which hold the whole universe enthralled" (p. 24).

4. Nelson Baker, in his book *You Can Understand the Bible by Its Unifying Themes,* makes the assertion that the most basic themes presented—Genesis through Revelation—include:

- God's desire for relationship with man,
- the inheritance he has provided (from Eden to the kingdom of heaven),
- man's continued "falls" from grace, and
- God's continued pursuit of reconciliation with man.

5. Nuclear fission is a process of division that releases enormous amounts of energy and deadly waste products. It can be created by man. Nuclear fusion is a process of reconciliation. It, too, releases enormous amounts of energy—clean energy. It cannot be fully duplicated by man.

6. If compassion deficits are a primary problem for our psyche, reconciliation to a God who is love, is the primary solution.

SCRIPTURE TO CONSIDER

1. Reconciliation occurs through the work of Jesus.

But now in Christ Jesus you who once were far away have been brought near through the blood of Christ. For he himself is our peace, who has made the two one and has destroyed the barrier, the dividing wall of hostility, by abolishing in his flesh the law with its commandments and regulations. His purpose was to create in himself one new man out of the two, thus making peace, and in this one body to reconcile both of them to God through the cross, by which he put to death their hostility (Ephesians 2:13-16, NIV).

2. All this is from God, who reconciled us to himself through Christ and gave us the ministry of reconciliation; that God was reconciling the world to himself in Christ, not counting men's sins against them. And he has committed to us the message of reconciliation (2 Corinthians 5:18-19, NIV).

3. We are instructed by Jesus to forgive and become reconciled to others.

> If he sins against you seven times in a day, and seven times comes back to you and says, 'I repent,' forgive him."The apostles said to the Lord, "Increase our faith! (Luke 17:4-5, NIV).

4. Reconciliation to others is of primary importance.

> Therefore, if you are offering your gift at the altar and there remember that your brother has something against you, leave your gift there in front of the altar. First go and be reconciled to your brother; then come and offer your gift (Matthew 5:23, 24, NIV).

USUAL AND UNUSUAL RESOURCES

1. *Men Are from Mars, Women Are from Venus,* by J. Gray. (New York: HarperCollins).

2. *Fit to Be Tied,* by B. & L. Hybels. (Grand Rapids: Zondervan Publishing House).

3. *Abba's Child: The Cry of the Heart for Intimate Belonging,* by Manning, B. (Colorado Springs: NavPress).

4. *The Return of the Prodigal Son,* by H. Nouwen. (New York: Image Books, Doubleday).

5. *Forgive and Forget,* by Lewis Smedes. (New York: Pocket Books).

ACTIVITIES FOR GROUP AND HOMEWORK

Group:

1. Pass around *The Return of the Prodigal Son* by Nouwen. Its cover is a reprint of Rembrandt's "Prodigal Son." Ask the group to share their feelings concerning the picture. With whom do they most identify?

2. Read the story of the Prodigal Son as captured by Eugene Peterson in *The Message.* Allow discussion.

3. Show the final scene of "God Views" (video by Cloninger described in book and under the "Leap Two ... " section of this appendix). It's another telling of the Prodigal Son story.

4. Hand-out pencils and paper and let all group members draw "maps" of their salvation history—from Egypt back to the Promised Land. Let them talk about the importance to their journeys of reconciliation.

Homework:

1. Assign any of the above mentioned resources for a weekly read-and-journal activity.

2. Send members to find a video clip that best shows someone going through a reconciliation scene that he feels he most needs.

3. Ask each member to bring in a CD or cassette tape which contains a song he would be willing to play for the group which communicates the message of reconciliation. Ask him where he is with this on a personal level.

Appendix B

Help Suggestions
from the First Three Helpers

In an attempt to tell about the hermit's suggestions for personal Christian formation, the very legitimate help offered by the first three helpers may seem minimized. So I thought I'd let them get a few of the last words in. What follows in this appendix is behavioral, cognitive, and "re-framing" suggestions which are keyed to common areas of emotional pain.

I. THE FIRST HELPER: CHANGING BEHAVIOR

A. LOW SELF-ESTEEM
    1. Spend fifteen minutes each day meditating on
texts that proclaim God's love and care for you.
For example:
      a. Luke 11:1-13
        … how much more will the heavenly Father give the
        Holy Spirit.
      b. Luke 12:22-34
        Lilies of the field … you are much more precious.
      c. Isaiah 43:1-4 & 49:14-16
        If you go through the fire I will be with you … you are
        precious in my eyes … I have carved you on the palms
        of my hands.
      d. Hosea 11:1-4
        When Israel was a child, I loved him.

e. Psalm 23

The Lord is my shepherd ...

f. Psalm 121

The Lord is your guardian and protector ...

g. Psalm 91

He will cover you with his wings; you will be safe in his care; his faithfulness will protect you.

h. Psalm 131

A prayer of trust ... as a child in its mother's arms ...

i. Romans 8:31-39

If God is for us who can be against us?

j. Matthew 10:29-31

Every hair on your head has been counted.

B. DEPRESSIONS

1. Make a list of twenty things that you greatly enjoy doing (e.g., walks alone, newspaper and coffee in the morning, doing something special for someone who is not expecting it, etc.). Then make it a personal priority to do at least two of these activities each day.

2. Make it a point to exercise at least one-half hour a day. Find the activity that is most enjoyable and start with it.

C. STRESS AND ANXIETY

1. Turn routine sources of stress (such as telephone rings or red lights when in a hurry) into mini-vacations. Let these events become signals to take a long, deep, slow breath. You might find yourself hoping the light will turn red or that the phone will ring.

2. Purchase an audiotape of a relaxation exercise. Set aside at least twenty minutes each day to relax while listening to the tape.

3. Take at least forty mini-vacations each day—slow, deep breaths.

4. Make a point to regularly clear one day to be completely free from any work/school activities. Make it a day that is away from the community and make sure the day is not Monday—you are too tired to relax on Monday—go to work.

D. ANGER
1. Relaxation is the best behavioral change you can make. Tell yourself, "I'm letting it (the hurt or anger) go" as you breathe out.
2. Count to ten—a tried and true intervention.
3. Cultivate one confidant with whom you can share your hurts and frustrations. At least once a month meet with this individual to let off steam. Confidentiality is a must.

E. THE FAMILY
1. Schedule a family night on your weekly calendar. Guard it religiously as a special time for family recreation and sharing.
2. Have a date with your spouse each week. Dress up for it.
3. Give your spouse at least one hour each week when all you do is listen. If you have to use tape on your mouth, use it.

II. THE SECOND HELPER: CHANGING THOUGHT PATTERNS

A. LOW SELF-ESTEEM
1. Talk back to your internal critic.
   a. Train yourself to recognize and write down the self-critical thoughts as they go through your mind.
   b. Learn the patterns of thoughts and how they are distorted.

  c. Practice talking back to them in order to develop a
     more realistic self-evaluation.

B. DEPRESSION
  1. Don't take criticism as a personal put-down. Ignore all
     unsigned critical letters. You make the evaluation. Is the
     criticism valid? If so, give praise for the free advice. If not,
     put it in the round file cabinet.
  2. Make a list of your temporal "losses" and disillusion-
     ments. Share this list with your spouse or a trusted friend.
     Grieve the losses until there are no more tears. The
     depression should lift.

C. STRESS AND ANXIETY
  1. Make it a habit to say no to events and schedules which
     are not consistent with your personal mission statement
     ("rule of life"). Do not even entertain any thoughts
     about guilt when you have done the above.
  2. List and argue with your thoughts that tell you that you
     must be perfect, busy, or constantly active to be approved
     of. Dare to be average. Remember, it is not you but God
     who is doing the work. Think: "I am letting God be my
     press agent."

D. ANGER
  1. When angry, remind yourself of the following:
     • Events don't make you angry. Your "hot thoughts"
       create your anger. Don't replay them.
     • Most of the time your anger will not help you. It will
       immobilize you and drown you in your own hostility.
     • Your thoughts that generate anger always contain dis-
       tortions. Let your spouse or a close friend help you
       find and correct the distortions.

- Try to see the "hot situation" through the eyes of the other. His actions may not seem unfair from his point of view.

F. THE FAMILY

1. Expect to invest a great deal of time and energy in your relationships. Lasting relationships don't just happen.
2. Remember, if you take time to talk with your family members each day, you will never become strangers.
3. Write down all the reasons why you love each person in your family. Then, when the going gets rough, take the list out and reread it. It resolves problems quickly (L. Buscaglia).

III. THE THIRD HELPER: CHANGE OF PERSPECTIVE

A. LOW SELF-ESTEEM

1. Value yourself. Then, after you value yourself, be willing to clean the shoes of another.
2. Remember that the least of those who play outside the cave are better off than the most astute and honored shadow interpreter.

B. DEPRESSION AND ANXIETY

1. Remember that you are not of the world. You do not have to compete for and win the laurels—the badges of success—that the world hands out. No amount of striving or attaining can make you feel safe and secure. No amount of accumulating and collecting of honors or degrees can make you happy.
2. In the invisible, upside-down kingdom, we are called to let go of, not hold on to; to empty ourselves, not fill

ourselves up. Lie back in the boat, enjoy the breeze, trust that the current will take you home.

C. ANGER

1. Learn to separate the feeling from the behavior. That is, "be angry and sin not."
2. A great deal of your anger involves your defense against loss of self-esteem when people criticize you. Remind yourself of your place in your Father's kingdom and of his love for you as his child.
3. Mentally practice the two-by-four example. Remember not to forgive too soon or too late.
4. Remind yourself of God's design to forgive you.
   - Isaiah 55:1-13
     You who are thirsty come ... God is generous in forgiving.
   - Luke 15:11-32
     The Prodigal Son.
   - Psalm 103
     No less that the height of heaven is the greatness of his love.
   - 2 Corinthians 5:17-21
     ... for our sake God made the sinless one into sin.
   - Luke 5:1-10
     Parables of the lost sheep and the lost coin.
   - John 10:7-18
     I am the good shepherd who lays down his life for his sheep.
   - 1 John 1:5-2:2
     If we acknowledge our sins, he who is just can be trusted to forgive us.
   - Romans 8:28-39
     Is it possible that he who did not spare his own Son

would not be on your side?
- Revelation 7:9-17
He will lead them to life-giving water.

D. THE FAMILY

1. Compare the values which you place on each of the major areas of responsibility or activity in your life (spouse, children, career, devotion time, recreation or personal development). Then compare the value which you feel you place on each area with the amount of time you actually spend each week attending to that area. Spend time in prayer and meditation regarding any significant discrepancies.

Appendix C
Scripture Themes

True and False Selves
Jn 12:24-26; Rom 7:15-24; 6:3-11; Col 3:10-11; 2:11-12; Phil 3:7-16; Mk 8:34-38

Eight Leaps Home
Kingdom
Mt 4:23; 6:33; 9:35; 13:18-23, 23-35; 25:1-13; Mk 4:26-29; Lk 4:43; 17:31; 16:16; 13:18-21; 14:28-32; Rom 14:17; I Cor 15:24; Col 1:13

Practicing the Presence
Dt 4:29-31; Mt 25:31-46; 26:26-30; 28:18-20; Lk 24:13-35; Col 1:26-29; Jn 14:23; 1 Cor 6:19-20; 2 Cor 13:3-5; Jos 1:9; Ex 13:20-22

Listening to God
Jer 7:22-28; 20:7-13; 31:3; Jn 14:20-22; Hos 2:21-22; Ps 63:1-8; Jn 10:1-10; Heb 3:7-13; Mt 7:21-27; Lk 11:27-28; Is 50:4-5; Jer 7:1-11; Mk 4:1-20; 17:1-8; Jn 10:27-30; Lk 10:23-24; Ps 37:3-7; Jn 5:36-47; Rom 10:14-21; Is 43:1-2; Rv 3:13-22

Willingness
Hos 14:2-10; Col 3:12-15; Lk 6:46-49; Mt 16:21-26; Lk 14:7-11; Gal 2:19-21; Lk 14:28-33; Jn 13:33-35; Mt 19:27-30; Ex 13:20-22; Lk 18:18-27; Jn 21:18-22

Fears and Idols to Overcome
Ps 62:5-8; Mt 6:25-34; Ps 142; 27:10-14; Heb 13:5b-9; Ps 111; 43:3-5

Our Own Personal Cross
Lk 5:1-11; Mt 19:27-30; Lk 9:57-62; Lk 18:18-27; Eph 5:1-2; Heb 2:9-18; 2 Cor 4:16-18; Mk 14:32-42; 2 Cor 1:3-7; Gn 50:18-21; Is 25:4-9

Forgiveness
Lk 57:14-19; Neh 9:15-31; Mt 5:43-48; Lk 23:33-43; 1 Jn 2:3-11; 4:16-21; Mt 5:23-26; 5:9; 1 Pet 3:8-12; Lk 11:1-4; Mt 18:21-35; Eph 4:25-32

Reconciliation
Rv 7:13-17; Mt 6:9-15; Eph 2:12-16; Jn 20:19-23; 1 Cor 13:4-7; Gn 45:1-15; Lk 17:3-4; Ps 32; 1 Jn 1:6-10

Institute of Clinical Theology (ICT)

The Institute of Clinical Theology was born of a deep desire to promote efforts which systematically pursue an interdisciplinary understanding of Christian change and transformation.

The terms "clinical theology" were chosen and placed together to infer the application of practical and devotional theology in clinical settings. Implied in this infrequent juxtaposition is the desire to simultaneously borrow from the methodology of applied psychology (the scientific method and diagnostic nomenclature) and the content areas of theology (specifically Christian formation).

Since 1992 the ICT has sponsored post-graduate course work in Christian formation and spiritual direction for mental health professionals and pastoral counselors. Additionally, a variety of research and clinical service activities have been undertaken.

ICT's Board of Reference includes: Donald Aultman, David Benner, Gary R. Collins, Richard Foster, Donald Harris, Roger Hurding, Richard Gorsuch, Carey Merritt, H. Newton Malony, John Ortberg, Leanne Payne, Siang-Yang Tan, and Dallas Willard.

For more information about the ICT or to reach Gary Moon please write:

Institute of Clinical Theology, at
Psychological Studies Institute
2055 Mount Paran Road, N.W.
Atlanta, Georgia 30327
or call
Phone: (404) 233-3949, x 110

LifeSprings Resources

2425 WEST MAIN ST., P.O. BOX 9
FRANKLIN SPRINGS, GEORGIA 30639

LifeSprings Resources is a ministry of the International Pentecostal Holiness Church, a denomination committed to reaching the world with the message of Jesus Christ. LifeSprings provides Christian books, Sunday School curriculum, magazines, training materials, and other supplies to churches of many denominations across the United States and around the world. The ministry also provides custom printing services to churches and other religious organizations, as well as commercial printing services to a variety of business entities. Whether providing resources to churches or printing custom materials for a church or business, LifeSprings Resources' goal is to deliver top quality products and outstanding customer service in the most efficient way possible. For more information call 1-800-541-1376.

Notes

TWO
Adam and the Three Unhelpful Helpers

1. No, I did not get this from Lewis Grizzard's book, *If Love Were Oil, I'd Be About A Quart Low* (Atlanta: Peachtree Publications, 1983).
2. Norman Cousins best-seller, *Head First: The Biology of Hope,* (New York: Penguin, 1990) is one example of the effort to document strides in mind-body research. Many leading medical schools, such as those at Harvard and UCLA, are including mind-body research in their course offerings.
3. Jacob Needleman, *Money and the Meaning of Life* (New York: Doubleday, 1991), 94-96.
4. In my opinion many psychologists and philosophers have described the internal tug-of-war between the false and true selves, using a variety of different labels. Jung (described in the 1975 edition of his *Letters,* 2) views spiritual growth as the dethroning of the ego as the center of personality and the coronation of the self as that center. David Benner (1988) in his book *Psychotherapy and the Spiritual Quest* discusses the work of Fritz Kunkel and his development of an explicitly religious psychology in which spiritual growth is seen as a process of self-transcendence (the transcendence of the egocentric self by a we-centered self). John Finch uses similar language as Thomas Merton in talking about the suffocation of the *imago dei* by our false self. Leanne Payne in *Restoring the Christian Soul through Healing Prayer* deals extensively with the concepts of true and false selves, while providing some needed correctives for viewing the theology of Jung. Additionally, James Finley in Merton's *Palace of Nowhere* devotes considerable attention to Merton's conceptualizations of a true and false self.
5. Needleman, 127.
6. Dallas Willard, *The Spirit of the Disciplines,* (San Francisco: Harper & Row, 1988), 91.
7. See Oden, T. (1984). *Care of Souls in the Classic Tradition,* ed. D.S. Browning (Philadelphia: Fortress Press, 1984).
8. See Larry Crabb's book *Inside Out* for a broad treatment of this theme (Colorado Springs: NavPress, 1988).

9.   For more about this I would recommend Rebecca Propst's article, Cognitive-behavior therapy, in *Baker Encyclopedia of Psychology*, edited by David Benner (Grand Rapids, Mich.: Baker, 1985).

10. Rabbi Kushner, *When Bad Things Happen to Good People* (New York: Avon, 1981).

11. See Heidegger's chapter "Being and Time." Published in 1962 by Harper & Row in a volume edited by J. Macquarrie and E. Robinson.

THREE
The Hermit and the Eight Giant Leaps

1.   This story is a paraphrased version of a longer, and better told edition by Doc McConnell, called "The Walkin' Catfish." It has been published in *Best-Loved Stories: Told at the National Storytelling Festival* (Jonesborough, Tennessee: National Storytelling Press, 1991), 21-22.

2.   John Bright, *The Kingdom of God* (Nashville: Abingdon, 1990), 10.

3.   This reference is to a series of audio tapes titled *The Gospel of the Kingdom of Heaven*. Dr. Willard is currently completing a book on the same theme.

4.   John V. Taylor, *The Go-Between God* (Philadelphia: Fortress, 1979).

5.   Gerald May, *Will and Spirit* (San Francisco: Harper & Row, 1982), 91.

6.   May, 6.

7.   Willard, 9.

8.   M. Scott Peck, *The Road Less Traveled* (San Francisco: Touchstone, 1980), 17. See also *Collected Works of C.G. Jung,* (Princeton, N.J.: Princeton University Press, 1973). In R.F.C. Hull trans. Vol. II, *Psychology and Religion, West and East*, p. 78.

FOUR
Shoestrings and Plastic Trophies

1.   Bernie Siegal, *Love, Laughter, and Miracles* (New York: Harper & Row, 1986).

2.   M. Scott Peck, *People of the Lie* (San Francisco: Touchstone, 1985), 60.

FIVE
The Last Major Detour

1. Archibald Hart, *Adrenaline and Stress* (Dallas: Word, 1991).
2. Much of the content of these lectures have since been published in a book by Peter Lord titled *Hearing God* (Grand Rapids: Baker, 1988).
3. Many would agree with the minister. Bernard J. Tyrrell, in *Christotherapy II,* (New York: Paulist, 1982) observes that there are four contemporary approaches to effective healing and growth in the human psyche. He labels these: exclusively spiritual, materialist, separate specialization, and the spiritual-psychological. Of these approaches, the minister was operating out of either the exclusively spiritual (the only valid avenue to wholeness is spiritual), or the separate specialization (ministers and psychotherapists have separate, non-overlapping areas of expertise and practice). While I had no helpful label at that time, in retrospect I was beginning to operate in the area Tyrrell would label, spiritual-psychological (the approach which seeks to integrate the principles and healing methods of psychology and psychiatry with those of a particular religion or spirituality—Christian spiritual direction in this case—into a higher synthesis which is both theoretical and practical).

SIX
Hummingbirds and Light Switches

1. Moses Maimonides, in *The Guide for the Perplexed,* makes the observation that the more necessary a thing is for living beings, the more easily it is found and the cheaper it is. Conversely, the less necessary an object is, the rarer and dearer it is (i.e., air and water versus diamonds and gold).
2. Leanne Payne, *The Healing Presence* (Grand Rapids, Mich.: Baker, 1995), 23.
3. Peter Lord, *Hearing God* (Grand Rapids: Baker, 1988).
4. Lewis Smedes, *Forgive and Forget* (San Francisco: Harper, 1984).

SEVEN
Reconciliation: This Time It's Personal

1. Smiley Blanton, *Love or Perish* (New York: Simon and Schuster, 1956).
2. Philip St. Romain, *Becoming a New Person: Twelve Steps to Christian Growth* (Liguori, Mo.: Liguori, 1992).
3. T.E. Lawrence, *Seven Pillars of Wisdom* (Mattituck, N.Y.: Amereon, 1976).
4. Robert Munsch, *Love You Forever* (Buffalo, N.Y.: Firefly, 1986).

5. Ari L. Goldman, *The Search for God* (New York: Ballantine, 1992), 28.
6. Tony Campolo, Jr., *The Power Delusion* (Wheaton, Ill.: Victor, 1987), 11.
7. Campolo, 15.
8. Blanton.
9. Paul Tillich, *Courage to Be* (New Haven, Conn.: Yale University Press, 1959).

Epilogue

1. Rebecca Propst, *Psychotherapy in a Religious Framework: Spirituality in the Emotional Healing Process* (New York: Human Sciences Press, 1988).
2. Nelson B. Baker, *You Can Understand the Bible* (Philadelphia: A.J. Holman, 1973).